A
COURSE
IN CHRIST

Jesus Reminds Us
Who We Truly Are

Scribed by
Alice Friend

A COURSE IN CHRIST

The poem, 'THE GREETING' from
© The Gifts of God by Helen Schucman, paperback fourth printing 2008
reproduced with kind permission by the copyright holder and publisher,
The Foundation for Inner Peace.

Cover photo by © Alice Friend
Detail of sunrise from her roof in Spain

The Greeting

Say but "I love you" to all living things
And they will lay their blessings over you
To keep you ever safe and ever sure
That you belong to God and He to you.

What but "I love you" could the greeting be
Of Christ to Christ, Who welcomes but Himself?
And what are you except the Son of God,
The Christ Whom He would welcome to Himself?

by Helen Schucman
from the ' Gifts of God'

Introduction

My name is Alice Friend and I'm in my 70's. I am a mother, a grandmother, a wife, a songwriter, a medium, a counsellor, a writer, an artist and I have a life-long love of God. I have always been attracted to Truth. Witnessing the world around me when I was in my early teens, seeing the strange way it seems to operate and its craziness, I went down on my hands and knees and shouted to God, " I want the Truth". And I know, over 50 years later, that call was heard.

My husband, Rod, and I have been living here in Spain for almost 20 years and have been students and teachers of A Course in Miracles all that time. For many years we have hosted a weekly meditation and study group focused on The Course.

In 2010 I self-published an on-going conversation I had for two years with the Holy Spirit who came to me in the form of a bird, a dove. The book is called ' A Little Bird Told Me' and is available from Blurb. In 2014, inspired by the Holy Spirit, I created and self-published the Holy Spirit Wisdom Cards. There are 46 cards and a little booklet with inspirational words and prayers. These are available from me directly and have been translated into 5 languages. Then, in 2016, I self-published a book of poems, 'A Touch of Gold', dedicated to my Love for God, which is available from Amazon.

THE RECEIVING OF
A COURSE IN CHRIST

Recently, I was having my first session with a friend who is studying to be a Life Coach. She asked me what my goal was in our sessions together. I thought deeply and decided to go for my greatest goal or desire. .....the call to know who I truly am and to live it, then help others know and live it also. So many spiritual teachings say we have forgotten who we are, or we must become who we truly are. I felt a one-pointed desire for this knowing so I committed to that goal then and there with all of myself. Two days later I was 'called' to get out my notepad and the presence of Jesus Christ united with me. He invited me to write with Him. This is the first time that Jesus has obviously and openly shared through me. This book you have in your hands now is the result of my commitment to knowing myself, and its answer.

The first words from Jesus to me were, "Many people now write, speak and express in My Name. This is because My Name is Your own. When you own your own name, you identify with that part of yourself. What if your name was more than you think it is? What if My name was also yours? The 'what if' is not an 'if' but an 'is'. YOU ARE CHRIST.

You are Alice Christ like I Am Jesus Christ. There is Mary Christ, John Christ, Rod Christ, Ruth Christ and so on...... each and everyone has Christ as their name, their true identity.

This is your name. Yet it is much more than your name, it is your true Self recognized by your Self. Do you understand? Now we ask you to go beyond understanding to knowing. Know you are Christ. You are beyond the name. You are the Child of God and the name of the child of God is Christ. All are Christ. I (Jesus) showed you who you are by being who I am."

He told me then and there who I truly am and asked me to write for and with Him to help me to know my True Self. It has been easy, loving, flowing and deeply transformational for me to be writing with the loving partnership of my good friend and Elder brother, Jesus Christ. I never know from sentence to sentence what will flow out of my pen. I always write freehand in my notebook first, then type it out onto my computer. I just allow the union with Jesus to happen in the surrendering. He always 'shows up' and writes through my hand with great love, ease and poetic power.

After writing for quite a few weeks, I asked what this could be called, He answered immediately, "A Course in Christ". I thought at once, "Oh no, that's too much to ask, Jesus, that is like a A Course in Miracles and A Course of Love." "Sort of ", He said, "but much simpler. I have already said what I wanted to share in those teachings. This is your next step" .

The writing is for me first because I asked to know who I truly am and to become it. I am taking on the words, doing what is being asked.... namely, watching myself with the Watcher and then with the Overseer of everything, my Christ Self.

In this undertaking I am the scribe for Jesus, so what better way to spend my life than committing to this for my Self? I am unlearning, rewinding, surrendering and I am in great Joy as I receive these words. It is changing the way I perceive and think about everything. My commitment to who I truly am is coming to me in the form of this communication and it feels amazing.

I find by re-reading and re-reading this discourse that the energy and the power in it is helping me receive the Great Love and healing transformation that Jesus is inviting me to experience. Step by step, repeating over and over again in different words but saying the same thing in essence, Jesus is guiding me, loving me, uniting with me.

Together we have done this and I want to share my experience now with you. I asked to know who I truly am and this was given. Little did I know what I was asking for and what form the answer would take.

He asked me to call this A Course in Christ, and now I understand why. A 'course' is a path, a journey, a way, and these writings are exactly that, A Course in Christ......a course, a path, in my (and your) Christ Self. Jesus is my inspiration and guide in our mutual Christhood, all the way Home.

Alice Friend, Spain, 2019

Forward from Nathalie Feenstra, Alice's Life Coach.

When we started our coaching relationship I asked Alice, "What would be a good outcome for you from our coaching sessions?" She answered: "I want to know my True Self and be able to share with others how to know their True Self."

What a beautiful quest and what an unexpected response!

Within no time, much to our mutual surprise, Alice started writing as a channel for her True Self whom we now know as the Christ Self. It has been a blessing to me to have been part of this journey and I am very excited now that she will move on to publishing the manuscript in book form for the world to be able to receive the beautiful, simple and powerful messages that she has received from Jesus .

Because Alice gave herself permission to step fully into her Higher Self, I can now do this myself. She has shown me the way. I have read the text, and have experienced a deeper connection to my Higher or Christ Self. My life has changed. I have been able to let go of many of my ego tendencies to keep myself small and have been able to stand more fully in the light of my True Self. In this process I have learned to love myself more fully and seem to have stopped most of my inner judgements.

What a gift to us all! Giving ourselves permission to be our Christ Self. Truly powerful, magnificent, innocent and beautiful. I hope this writing finds its way into the hands of many people so they can fully embrace their Self and step into the Light of their True Self! For this is Self- Realization.

Nathalie Feenstra

(Certified yoga and meditation teacher, yoga therapist, reiki practitioner and transformational life coach.)

Editor's Note

My wife Alice and I are long-term students of A Course in Miracles, the book authored by Jesus and scribed by Helen Shucman continuously from 1965 till 1971. This has been the inspiration and foundation for Alice's channel to be open to the same author.

I have always respected and deeply trusted Alice's skills as a counsellor, past life regression therapist and medium but it was still a big surprise for both of us when the material of this book started coming from Jesus in early Spring 2018.

Alice is a very pure medium. This book has not been written to appeal to the intellectual aspect of mind. It is not an "about" book. It is simply presenting us with empowered words to trigger our ancient memory of our True Self and identity; and it came initially just for Alice because she asked to know the true nature of her Self and from this how to help others know the same for themselves.

My part has been simply to check over the text for punctuation, word order and syntax but apart from that to leave the text unaltered, and this I have done. However, while undertaking this I have felt the author speaking to me personally while addressing perennial questions of mankind and because of this I know that I am shifting in the process of self-inquiry. For example, Jesus emphasizes the age-old injunction to find moments of stillness and to practice being 'in the seat of the observer', watching motives and addictive thoughts without judgement. I am having to actually do this myself and can no longer rely on the intellect by merely having read it.

The reader will notice that the style of the text is one of much repetition. This is, I believe, highly intentional and the outward sign of a supreme teacher who wants everyone 'in the class' to 'get it'. Another reason for the frequent repetition is that the book's central idea, that we are all the One Christ, seems a contradiction to the centuries of Christian doctrine so requires emphasis and reiteration. Certainly it is an idea whose time has come and represents a major step in human spiritual development.

The Christian religion has always taught that we are created in the image of our Creator and the words in this book, coming from Jesus, can help us all to no longer just pay lip service to this idea but to get 'joyfully serious' about actually living it.

Rod Friend
Spain, 2019

Contents

PROLOGUE BY JESUS

Page   Chapter

A COURSE IN CHRIST
PROLOGUE BY JESUS

Many people now write, speak and express in My Name. This is because My Name is Your own. When you own your own name you identify with that part of yourself. What if your name was more than you think it is? What if My name was also yours? The 'what if' is not an 'if' but an 'is'. YOU ARE CHRIST. You are Alice Christ like I Am Jesus Christ. There is Mary Christ, John Christ, Rod Christ, Ruth Christ and so on...... each and everyone has Christ as their name, their true identity.

This is your name. Yet it is more than your name, it is your true Self recognized by your Self. Do you understand? Now we ask you to go beyond understanding to knowing. Know you are Christ. You are beyond the name. You are the Child of God and the name of the Child of God is Christ. All are Christ. I , Jesus, showed you who you are by being who I am.

You need not in any way pay for or earn that which you are, your Christ identity. You need only to accept your Self. That Self is present in you anyway whether you accept it or not. Each of you has lived in a state of denial for a very long time and the time of denial has ended. The Light shines on what is true. The truth is who you are. You are Christ. You always have been and you always will be. As you really know this you use your eyes to see the Christ in everyone. This is Heaven's Sight. This is waking up to who you truly are.

I am here as a reminder and now is the time. So, dear Christ, as you write this with your authorship know all is at peace within you and may Light be your guidance.

In earlier times, to say ' I am Christ' would have been seen as blasphemous, but what is blasphemy? And how has it been used? It has been used by the Liar as with so many other things you have believed, to keep you anaesthetized or asleep to who you really are. The Liar is our name for the illusionary ego voice which has misrepresented you and your awareness of yourself and everyone else. Every One else. Every One Self. Every Self in Oneness, in wholeness of their Christ essence.

The Liar is now exposed. The great lie is exposed. There can be no punishment for Truth for in Truth there is only Light. The Light shines from, on and in Truth. The Light of You, Christ, is now shining from, on and in you.

You are baptised in the name of your Self, from Self and by Self. The inner eye, the Inner I, is clear and sees what it sees from its own Christ Light within.

Sight and Light are one. Sight happens when Light is shone and Truth is recognized. The Light of Truth shines on your Christ Self. This is not a future awareness. This is now. This is the Power of Now, the power of Love's awareness, Love's identity. Your identity..... the Christ Self.

' I Am the Light of the world'.

I shine on my Self and know who I Am.

You are I Am.

I Am you.

Christ I Am.

I Am says Christ within me.

I Am shines throughout me.

I Am surrounds me,

I Am.

1   JOY

Your true Self is Joy. It is unbounded, exalted joy. Joy in everything, everywhere, inside and out. In fact, inside is the home of joy. Inside your heart and inside your heart's eyes, ears, perception and awareness. Your heart's joy extends itself to all parts of you as breathing in oxygen penetrates every cell of your blood. Joy is your birthright. You know that you know who you are when you live in constant joy. This starts with a choice, a willing choice to laugh at everything, with everything and really 'see' all of life for what it is...... a celebration of the extension of Love and Its creation.

You have witnessed those whose joy has filled a room, radiated a space, touched your painful mind and put everything in perspective. Joy shines a light on all that is real, true and eternal and it cannot acknowledge what is a lie, a miserable game of self deceit and self-inflicted mind stories of self-loathing, tragedy, or other self-harming thoughts. Joy is who you are and what you are here to experience. It is your loving essence.

If you remember me or knew me you would remember my Joy. I laughed a lot and those close to me laughed with me. Through joy and laughter I saw and experienced what is real and was able to show others Reality. It is a joy to be with whoever knows and reveals the lightness of being. The Joy I am, the Joy I give, the Joy I am alive in is also your Joy. It is your celebration of knowing yourSelf, your life and your eternal spirit.

At times in your life you have met those who seem to laugh at everything, those who are in the Joy that lightens everything and everyone. (Tibetan monks have been known for this..... it is why they giggle at everything!) There is a saying, " You can go to the depths of hell and if you laugh, nothing can touch you". This is so, my beloved, this is so. What can hurt you when you laugh at it? What can influence you negatively when you see through it with the eyes of Joy? Joy is the greatest medicine, the healer of all ailments, the bringer of true abundance.

You can choose Joy right now. Truly choose it. Close your eyes and imagine me in front of you. If you cannot picture me as a figure, see me as a being of the Light I Am. Feel a touch upon your third eye. A strong touch of Light that travels through your whole being like an electric shock of Light. Let it penetrate all of you, inside and outside. Let it travel behind your eyes so your sight is affected. Let it travel within your ears so your hearing is affected. Let it travel to your heart so the very engine of your body is made anew and wakes you. Let it penetrate your mind where the light of Joy truly transforms and affects everything else. Joy is moving every part of you and your spirit celebrates because it is finally acknowledged and held and hugged and loved by you. Your spirit, your joyous spirit, which has always been and always will be the true eternal you, is exposed to you.

You are Spirit eternal.   You are Love eternal.

You are Light eternal.

You are Joy eternal . And now you know.

There is a deep, deep peace that comes from joy. An eternal smile of being at Home. Truly at Home. Being at Home in the Heaven you are created from is the joy I speak of and reveal to you. Be with me in this peace, in this joy and be totally with your Self at last. Your true Christ Self. Your joyous, peaceful Christ Self. Yes and yes and yes again because the dream of sleep, of deception, of the Lie is dissolved away in the Joy of true awareness.

Being in Joy does not mean that the experiences you have, be they shocking and painful or deeply loving and moving are not felt by you. However, now you know that moving through all your experiences is something greater than that which is temporarily affecting you. Eternal Joy is your constant companion.

These are not just words, for I am using words imbued with power. The power of Truth, of awakening, of Light. I am using words like a wand of awakening, touching your awareness so it is transformed. Your own ability to choose is your wand, and you all own your wand..... your choice. Use it on yourself, then watch its effects.

Many of the fairy tales of old tell of a journey. They tell of a wise one, a magic wand, a transformation, a waking up and then living in eternal happiness ("..... and they lived happily ever after") Many of these stories have been inspired by beings who knew themselves and wished the reader through the story, to remember their true Self.

To read stories like this to a child will keep awake a deep knowing within the child of their Real Self. The stories are not mere fantasy, they are real, my beloved. It might be a renewal for you to re-read some of the classic fairy tales and then extend them in your inner knowing to what I have shared here. You are living as the hero of your own awakening and you will live happily ever after.

....

2   CONTROL

To experience the joy we speak of, there are feelings and emotions that must be moved through and eliminated. As A Course in Miracles is a mind training to eliminate the blockages in the way of Love, you must eliminate everything in the way of Joy as well. This means no denial.

"But what is it that I deny?", you may ask. Even though you know something of yourself, you have much of yourself buried deeply in unconscious caverns and hidden places within you. Old hiding places that even you have forgotten about are covered up through fear and buried memories, shocks and heartbreaks that need to be freed. To be freed is a key here, because they are stuck. I am not just referring to this incarnation but to many past ones too. So, how do you free and heal hidden emotions to make way for the vastness of Joy's embrace? You let go of control.

Control is the basis for so much fear, anger, stuckness and sadness. It is an endless cycle until it stops. There seems to be an attachment to the fear that manifests as control in your life. Your need for control, either consciously or unconsciously, is holding back much in the way of Joy's expression, in the way of Love's expression. When you are in Joy, your ability to Love is unbounded. It is the other way around too. When you are in Love your ability to be an expression of Joy is unbounded.

Control can be subtle or obvious and often both. " No, I can't. No I don't believe this. No, it is too difficult. I won't, I can't, I am afraid to, I am unable to". Then there is the " No you can't. No you won't, you don't believe that! You don't have the skills to do that." These statements are for yourself or someone else. You can add to them. You know all about it, you know them well. What would happen if 'I can' and more often saying 'yes' became your norm? A willingness to be open-minded, not closed and rigid. The more control you need and have, the more rigid you are and the more easily you feel that you could or would lose control.

Truly joyous souls have let go of control. They have let go of opinions, judgements and attachments. They are truly free. Control can be hidden and very protected. To find the hidden fixed beliefs that make control dominate your life you must observe yourself. You live your life seemingly as only one part of you which is at the mercy of inward and outward experiences and circumstances.

However, there are also other parts of you. Let me introduce you to the Watcher. Who is it that you observe yourself with? And Who is witnessing that? These are vital questions to shifting control patterns. Watch yourself, observe your emotions, question them and then choose them or not. This is the ancient and effective practice of what has been termed 'self inquiry'. However, the stuck part of you does not want this to happen. The liar in you denies it all. Are you truly joyous all the time? Does your heart wake up in exultation at the light of a new day and give it spontaneous expression to a Source that always knows what is exactly right and true for you?

Watch, watch, watch...... observe, observe, observe...... No judgements, just watch. Get in the habit of watching your emotions, your behaviour and where it originates, and then choose. Choice is one of your greatest gifts. You even control your ability to choose. You think you can choose this but not that. You can choose everything. You can choose to be sad, to be depressed, to be a victim or you can choose to be happy, free and a creator of your life. You have the power within you, no matter what your circumstances.

You might have heard all this before from teachers and writings and self-help books. It is an important truth. Joy is a choice, a choice to let go of all control. Joy is the great treasure hidden under eons of hidden and stuck emotions. Just be the watcher of your life instead of the controller of it. Then choose. It takes a while to get into the habit of watching but soon it becomes second nature.

I watched myself. I stood outside of the me that seemed to be at the mercy of my environment, circumstances and others' need to control me. I knew who I was, who I Am and the unbounded and peaceful inner joy I felt about everything, even situations that seemed tragic. When I watch, I am not attached to anything. When there is no attachment there is no rigid control. Each experience, each moment of now simply is. This does not mean I had no compassion or feelings. It means I was not ruled by dramas or circumstances. I felt only Love and had vast inner space for that Love.

So, admit to yourself you have control patterns. Watch how you feel threatened when they are seen as dominating you in some way. Stand outside in your awareness of yourself and watch. Watch the effects that your addictions to sadness, sickness, judgements (especially towards yourself), guilt, opinions and fears have on your state of being. Your natural state of being is Joy and Love. All else is a false you. To be who you truly are...... Christ as an extension of God. Release all that is in the way of that.

Do you need help for this to happen? OK..... Ask. Ask and it is given. Pray, talk to me, talk to the Inner Higher Self Voice within you, the Holy Spirit, talk to your Creator. You are heard, you are listened to. 'I need help' is a wonderful admission. Control has to let go when you say that. I hope this is clear. It will be brought up again, for it is important.

A prayer:

" I come in need to give up control.
My God, help me see my control patterns and express Joy in my life.
Help me be Your Creation, my True Self,
the Christ being that You created.
I know in asking sincerely now for your help that all is dissolved that
is blocking my Joy. Thank you "

....

3   KNOWING GOD DIRECTLY

I have mentioned in other communications that the time of an intermediary between yourself and God is ending. This is because you are able to know God directly. In knowing God directly in Unity you know yourself. Do you need an intermediary to know yourself? You may do for a time (and that is only for remembering) but once you have remembered, there comes a time for that need to fall away. Any intermediaries are meant to fall away for you to unite with the Self that is you. Everything you are and need to know lives within you. It is just a matter of remembering, choosing and accessing this for yourself.

In a sense you might say that your parents are intermediaries in the early stages of your earthly life. When your body is just born it is helpless and needs to adjust to the world and to be looked after. You need to be taught to live in the world. Your true parent is God who has shown you for thousands and thousands of your years how to live in inner peace, what values to live by and which choices you can make to create a Heaven on Earth. But time and time again you have separated from the Laws of Love that created a peaceful and joyous life. You remember them in some deep, unconscious place within you as a memory of contentment, harmony and inner and outer abundance.

There is a misplaced desire in you for independence, experimentation, separateness and control. In this you seem to have 'thrown out the baby with the bathwater'. In other words, by seemingly separating from God you have struggled. You have thrown yourself out of Heaven. There have been many teachers, guides and techniques to remind you of Heaven, of constant peace and contentment. You have never really left, as it is alive within you. Now your desire to return is so great that you want nothing else. Now you may leave the intermediary, grow your own wings of knowing and Unity which have always been there but are finally remembered, and the dark cloud of separation can fall away so that clarity of mind, soul, body and wisdom can return.

You wonder if I am an intermediary here. I Am not an intermediary but your equal companion, accompanying you. I have already taken this journey, this course to know the Christ I Am. I am now with you as we join in our Christ Awareness. I will be referring to this more as we continue together.

Here I Am, Lord,
Talking to you directly as I remember
that I Am as You created me.
I commit to knowing my Christ Self
and honour Your Divine Love within me .

....

4   HEAVEN'S GARDEN

You are my equal brothers and sisters in our mutual Christhood. I hold your hands in great celebration and unity, and in a beautiful ring of love we dance the dance of re-union and celebration. I exalt in your homecoming as we are all here in our Father/Mother's Home and Garden united and truly together.

It is a great journey you have been on. An adventure to the realms of your inner world and the world of form. What souls you have met, what emotions you have experienced. You have been in and out of incarnations of the body many times. You have watched yourself in spirit, with and without a body, many times. You have made many choices and reaped the effects of your choices. You chose to come Home and your path was laid before you and illumined with the sparkles of the stars of Heaven.

You observed the world you lived in from many different perspectives as you walked upon your starry pathway Home. You met fellow travellers on the same path and paused with them a while to share food for the body and food for the soul. Then you continued, wondering all the time if what you chose was real. But you actually had no other choice and you knew this. You just delayed a while at times.

Your journey is also my journey. I know the starry path. I know the lures of the body and the world. I also know of your awareness of constant union with your Creator. You may have felt my footsteps in front of your own on the path. In fact, we met often without you recognizing me. I can walk that path still and take your hand when you are tired or in doubt. I can extend myself and walk with you on the journey to our common Home. You recognize your Self in me and I equally recognize my Self in you. We are One in the Christ Force of our Creator's lighted love.

Love is Light. Love and Light are united. You are the creation of this united Force and you never were not. You now may seem to be in the world still and yet I tell you that you are Home with me and all others. Know this Home in your heart as you go about everything in your life. I do not exclude your body and your life in your world. I do not condemn or judge it. I know it very well. You are in fact me, as I am living your journey.

It seems now there is a duality, the heavenly knowing and the worldly one. One you see with your physical eyes and one you see with your spirit's eyes. Yet in the seeming duality of this experience there is union. The union that defies understanding or definition, it just is. Allow me to unite and blend with you. Recognize your Self from my experiences that were and are your own. Feel the beating of my heart and know we are loving and uniting with all our brothers and sisters.

I laugh and smile with you as I watch and participate with you all, like the way you watch, smile and laugh when you are with a new baby who is discovering everything around it for the first time. As it experiences water, flowers, friendship, cuddles, kisses, bubbles. In wonder and trust the child touches life. In trust, all is well. I am playing in the garden of Heaven with you and we are our beloved Creator's children in wonder together.

From here, from Heaven's garden, you can watch yourself in your experience of incarnation as you live in the world. Now you know you are watching and where you watch from. Feel watched, feel observed, feel safe in your own Sight as you watch your self. It is your Christ Self watching you, your True Self at Home watching you. Blend with the sight of this in your heart and KNOW.

....

5   DIVINE LAW

Divine Law, what is it? The word 'law' can bring up defense in you, so let's clean that up first. Divine Law is full of principles or guidelines that work. Cause and effect.... if this is done, then that is the outcome. Let us use another word to define our meaning. Divine Direction. Does that sound easier? So, Divine Law is Divine Direction and Divine is of God.

God's Direction (Divine Law) has been given to you so you know how to choose from your Christ Identity so that in all situations peace and joy can be the outcome. There is absolutely no place whatsoever for fear or the liar (ego) to have any power within Divine Law because Divine Law is of Love, from Love and for Love. It is the natural way Heaven 'operates'. I am using words from your vocabulary and understanding to make a point that otherwise might not be fully understood.

Can you imagine the scenario of populating the planet Earth for the first time, not with cave men as you have been told, but by souls that were innocent, pure, beautiful, trusting, radiant and open? Even though they thought they had separated from Heaven, there was still the spark, the core of their unseparated Self within them. That core is the eternal seed of Truth, of course. From that Truth there is a vibration of harmony. In order to be in Harmony, a way of being, thinking, behaving, speaking and interacting is necessary. This way and this union with everything and everyone works with the application of Divine Law or Divine Direction.

When exposed to a totally new and alien environment, such as with new beings just born on planet Earth, guidance was necessary to show how life works perfectly in matter. All are embraced in the protective loving arms of Divine Law. This is still being given in love by the Angelic Presence as well as by 'visitors' from other dimensions, God's children. They came to guide and direct new beings living on earth while they felt temporarily separated from their Heavenly Home. You were shown the example of Divine Law and Divine Choice to create a truly joyous and easy life. This is your birthright, your inheritance to keep you in awareness of your Christ Essence so that you could reproduce Heaven on Earth! And my beloved, this happened for a time and is still possible. The vision and remembrance of this has never left any of you.

When fear, lack, mistrust, boundaries, separation and other contracted thoughts and emotions entered, Divine Law was forgotten and laws based on fear, not love, became the norm. This is what you witness now. You still have the Voice of Love present inside you to remind you of Heaven's ways and Heaven's harmony. The world you inhabit with your incarnated body is the result of your own actions and thoughts. I am sure you can see in your heart a world in complete harmony operating naturally from actions using the laws of Divine Love. You have this guidance system within you. It never left. You know within your innermost self what I am referring to.

When you can truly let go of your need for tight control inside you from a place of separation and can replace that with the soft and flexible, safe and loving guidance of your Creator who only wants your happiness, you are living who you truly are. Does this not stir excitement in your heart? Ahhhh..... you feel, breathing a huge sigh of relief. Now, my beloved, invite that feeling to float up to the surface of your awareness and become re-acquainted with it once again. Live and be in Divine Law, Divine Direction and watch your life work smoothly and easily, 'In the flow', so to speak. In the Divine flow as you live your Christ Self.

....

6   BEING AND DOING

I would like to share about the doing and the being parts of your life. In your doing life you are physically active as you do many things, visit places, see people and are practical with what the body is calling forth in you and the many doing activities. Much, but not all of the doing life is about your body, its experiences, its needs, what the senses give to it, where you go, where you have just been, eating and all that that entails, buying or growing food, preparing it and so on. Doing is an active part of your life which animates you and is mostly expressed outwardly.

It is interesting that you are called Human Beings because you could be called Human Doings. To do something, whatever it is, is felt as an accomplishment, a task well or not well done, to accomplish whatever it is that you want to experience. Doing is an activity and it takes some sort of effort, some sort of action. In a body, because of its very nature, action is paramount for it is created to perform action of some sort most of the time. This is one way that proof is given you that you are a living entity that moves and has a force that motivates you. Doing is part of your spirit and life force. It springs from a motivated part of you and creates accomplishments in whatever activity you undertake. Doing is one of the most used words in your language as well. To do or not to do, is that the question?

Now, being. What difference do you feel when the word being is introduced after the word doing? What happens to your inward state when being is mentioned? Where do you 'go' with that? Being with someone or something is a more inside job, so to speak. To be. To be what and who? Who are you being? Are you being who you truly are? If not, who are you being? If you are, then you know you are Christ.

You take your being with you wherever you are. Your being accompanies you throughout your whole existence in a body or out of one. Be still and contact your being now. Feel it, feel its force and its presence. Your being is responding to your attention, is it not? It almost speaks to you. It certainly communicates. What does it say? Maybe it would not use words that you are familiar with. Maybe it would hum or chant or show you an image or a feeling.

You are a human being. What does that really mean? 'To be or not to be.' Is that the question? To be what? You know by now that I am emphasizing throughout these discourses who you truly are, your essential being. You and I are being with each other during this time.

You are being with me and the awareness of me and I am being with you and the awareness of you. What and who is being with whom? And what are we being together?

As we join in our being together we unite as one being, one force, one presence and we feel something deep within. Our united heartbeats are the same pulse as the Source of our being. In being aware of that Source we vibrate together as one, in union with all that is. Now, visualize being with a tree or a flower or with nature. You somehow unite or blend with the tree, with the flower or with nature. Being helps you to be the witness to your Self. Being is witnessing. Just being...... just being.

Being and doing are different sides of the same coin. What does it mean with being on one side and doing on the other? Actually, it does not matter at all, it happens whether you are aware of it or not.

I just wanted to bring your attention today to the recognition of your doing and your being so that your awareness of both is more awake in you. Doing and being can often overlap too. Your being is doing whatever it is doing. Just observe this as you court with whom you truly are.

....

My beloved, today I want to take you to meet your Self. Take my hand in yours now and trust me. Let go of all excuses to mistrust. Let go of them now. Become like a little child in total surrender and confidence as your innocent hand extends and is held in my hand. We are one. We need each other to come into the awareness of One. We need each other equally. We fly together easily and naturally into the Light of Knowing.

Here we are in the light of Knowledge and Love. Here, also, is the great meeting hall of all souls created in the Light and Love of the One. The One extended Its own Oneness into unique qualities and you are One of those and so am I. Here you meet the Making of your creation. Ask your Created One to meet you now. Here It comes like a flowing, living, pulsing Essence whose Presence is like liquid light itself. Liquid Light that is able to transmit Its essence to the you who feels separated from it. A great peace surrounds you. You expected excitement, however a peace of deep knowing is what is given. The Peace of knowing, the Peace of safety and of relief. Your Light Self meets your self within your body. You need each other. You have longed for this reunion and for this melting with the Presence of your Immaculate Self. You are not separate. You never have been. You have only forgotten until now. You have forgotten that you are everything Light is, everything Love is, everything I am and everything you are. It is the same in the oneness of the One. You are as God created you and always have been.

Re-membering, re-uniting with your Self now opens you to the vastness of your life. Your whole life, with and without a body. In incarnation and out of it. There is total continuity no matter what seems to happen. There is total continuation because you are the extension of the Continuation Itself. Whatever continues, extends. In its extension it continually receives ItSelf. You continue to receive yourSelf as you relax into being you.

My hand holding yours has melted now and become the One hand of Ours at Home in Love. It is guiding your remembering, your union. There is no going back now. You are integrated and whole, united and at peace. Take this awareness with you always in your heart, the heart of your knowing. Peace is with you. The Peace of Your Self.

....

8   NO HIERARCHY

Dear one, I say to you that where I am coming from there is no hierarchy. There is no-one and nothing above or below another. We are all equal as one. There is succession but not hierarchy. This is important for you to grasp and embody in your knowing. Hierarchy is man-made, not God-made. A loving Creator would not create hierarchy for any purpose whatsoever. Above and below are not in any way in competition with each other. Neither is anything in between. Hierarchy exists only when the liar (the ego) is present.

In many organizations, systems and situations you have made hierarchies which you have taken for granted as the normal way of things. It is not the way of Heaven to have any hierarchy, therefore it is not of Love. You are all equal in the eyes of Love. Everything is. Just as the sun shines on everything and everyone equally so it is with Love. Love shines like the sun shines, it just shines its Great Light. It is up to you whether you stand in it or in the shadows it makes, but it continues to shine.

Look around at your world and see what seems to you to be normal and acceptable. Hierarchies are everywhere. In your mind especially. You have even created hierarchies in Nature as if Nature could be better or worse in itself. You have placed others below you or above you. You compare and separate and categorize. You act differently towards someone in a so-called high position than to someone in a so-called low position,

One thing that is not of the Spirit at all is the hierarchy that has been created and misused in religious organizations where you can give your power of choice to another who has put themselves in a position of authority above you. There is a saying: "Where there is a spark of the Holy Spirit, the ego (liar) comes and organizes it". What does it do when it organizes it? It creates hierarchy.

I was a rebel. I rebelled against the misuse of the gift of God power. God power is the Power of God, your Maker, your Creator, inspiring your life, your decisions, your intuition and sense of true knowing. This is misused when someone other than God takes the position of a higher god above you and makes you feel inferior so they can say that their place is greater than yours. God would never do that and it happens everywhere, in businesses, in homes, in religious institutions, in government. This is serious mismanagement of God's Holy Laws that make everything unfold as it is in Heaven. Hierarchy is not of Heaven. As long as you allow (and I use the word 'allow' on purpose here) hierarchy to exist in any form in your life you will not know your True Self or know Heaven on Earth.

Yes, it is necessary for those in positions of temporary authority to lead and organize in any given situation but only with the sole purpose to empower you, not to take any power from you. So do not put me above you. I am equal to you. So equal, in fact, that I Am you. Your Self is My Self and all Selves. In Heaven there is no need for any kind of structure or rules. The 'Golden Rule' is more than a rule and can be called the 'Golden Truth':

' Do unto others as you would have them do unto you'.

This is natural in Heaven. It is only in treating others how you would like to be treated that you see yourself as an equal part of the whole.

If you encounter, as you often do, someone in a situation that you may feel is 'below' you, how do you treat them, first in your mind, your thoughts, then in your actions? Do you perceive them as 'below' you? Do they perceive you as 'above' them? Is a servant below you? Is a master above you? Above what? If you were a servant, how easy would it be to serve your master as you would like to be served? If you were a master, how easy would it be to treat your faithful servant as you would like to be treated? Who is serving whom? And for what purpose? Think deeply on this, my beloved.

Your Creator is Unity, Love and Peace and sees every part of Creation as equal and as One. Therefore, there is the Golden Truth: Treat all as you would like to be treated. Give to all as you would like to be given to. Greet all as you would like to be greeted. Welcome all as you would like to be welcomed. Love all as you would like to be loved. This is the way of Love, the way of Heaven. There is no hierarchy in the Golden Truth.

When you know this, you know your Self. You know your Self as God knows you. Equal in all ways. This view of communication is very important in order for you to know Truth. Again I say, watch and observe. Just watch so you learn by witnessing what 'works' or what keeps you and your brothers and sisters from living in the state of Heaven.

There is no hierarchy. There is only equal love. Equality in perceiving others and all things as you would wish to be perceived. Now, bless. Bless with your eyes, your sight, your mind, your thoughts, your heart and your speech. Bless as you would want yourself to be blessed.   Blessed Be.

....

What comes from Me is what comes from the You that is the Me. I know this may sound like a riddle and may wash over your head as words not fully grasped or understood, far less taken on board. Much of what I share and say is taken like that. Nice words, profound phrases, deep meanings. But what of taking it in, taking it on board on your journey to the Presence of Heaven?

'What comes from Me is what comes from the You that is the Me.' Let me explain further. Even though the Truth of Unity and Oneness is not fully 'grasped' by you in your mind as yet, Unity and Oneness is Reality. So, in that Reality, what comes from Me through you is the You that is the Me. We are One in the One and from that One we are all One. Within that One there is individuation, not separation but individual expressions of the One. Unique expressions of the same One. The same Source. Look at a mother who has given birth to say, four children but each of the four is a unique expression from the same source of the two parents. Those four children are unique expressions, individuals, not separated from their parents or brothers and sisters. They are single but in Oneness with their family.

Do not feel that by fully accepting who you are as the Unity of All will deprive you in any way of anything. This is a big fear in all of you. In fully accepting your Oneness, (which is so whether you accept it or not) you will not 'lose' something of who you are. What, my beloved, could you possibly lose? You can never lose what you truly are. You can only gain from that full awareness.

I gained My Identity, my Christ Identity, which I already had, of course, but I gained the full awareness of it. This is what I am inviting and guiding you to do as well. What is happening is that you are letting go of control and of old ideas of your self that have not served you well. Even by simply reading these words the letting go process is happening. You know, deep within, who you are, what you are here to be and your true identity. You know. Truly know. What has been in the way of that knowing? Lies, untruths, fears and the mistaken idea you have about your unworthiness. What is unworthiness but a sleep state of false identity? Unworthy of being who you truly are. How ridiculous is that! From my point of view it is very strange that anyone could or would feel, or be made to feel that they are unworthy of being who they truly are.

How do I know I am worthy? By total surrender. TOTAL surrender. Do you not think I weighed up all the facts, all the proof, all the experiences from many lives before I gave up all that was in the way of Love's Presence? I thought I had to have proof, understanding and experiences like any of you but I finally saw through all these things as illusory blockages put in place by forgetfulness. If you forget something, where is it? It never left. You merely misused your memory. You do remember your Source. You do remember your Unity. You do remember who you are.

What or who is the prince that kisses the Sleeping Beauty? The 'Prince' is the Awakener within. The Awakener is you. You are the story of your own awakening. You kiss or rouse yourself into waking up to the Truth. Surrender is necessary because when all is said and done, that is all you can do. In surrendering you do not give up anything. Instead, you give yourself to Your Self. Finally and completely. This is why it is so important to let go of control. How can you surrender when you feel you need to keep control?

There is such a total relief when you surrender. You have experienced moments of surrender in situations in your life. I emphasize here, you lose nothing and gain everything. I know this and surrendering brings ultimate Peace. Of course it does. If you do not want Peace in your life, keep controlling, keep active in the battle against being your True Self, keep in a semi-depressed state, keep sleeping in a glass coffin closed off from the Truth. Let me be your 'Prince'. You certainly are sleeping to your Great Beauty, your Light, your Identity. I 'kiss' your Christhood with my own, and then you 'kiss' others. We need each other to awaken and then joyously dwell in the Peace of Heaven together.

....

10   **FREE WILL**

As you move towards remembering more and more you move towards your Self. As to a strong magnet you are attracted to your Self. Once you know you are on the way, there is no turning back. It is impossible to turn back to your old state of sleeping or unawareness now that you are calling your self towards your Self. Once heard, the call cannot go unheeded. You are drawn towards Love, your Home. There is no greater mission or purpose in your life than to become who you truly are. To rediscover and unite with your Self, to remember what you have never lost but only forgotten.

Everything in your life is now subtly but profoundly changed. An upside down world has righted itself again. Nothing is perceived as it was and can never be again. Your glimpses of everything are viewed seemingly from your same 'eyes' but the way you see is clearer, sweeter, calmer, more loving and joyous and from sight that knows all is in unity and not in separation.

More and more of you are experiencing this. You are not alone. There is a wave of Great Love flowing through everyone now. It may not seem that way when you read or watch the news. On the 'outside' the dramas of life are being played out faster and faster. On the inside however, life is unfolding more peacefully with the awareness of Love's Presence in everything.

Children are being born already knowing themselves and you are increasingly in awe of the confidence, wisdom and awareness of many young people. They know the world they chose to be born into is now transforming and they have no tolerance for lies, hypocrisy, unfairness and false teaching. It is happening very fast now. There is a shift in the 'poles' of the way you perceive everything.

I am with you, guiding your every move, your thoughts, your choices. You have invited me and I am here. I am more available than ever before because there is an awakening to Love's Presence and Love's Recognition. You have heard of the second coming. The second coming of who and what? The second coming of Christ is your awareness of your own Christ nature. You are the second coming of Christ in unity, wholeness and Oneness with all. Do you feel it? Do you witness what I speak of? Do you witness? I am not only your guide. I am your Self. The I Am is you and who is writing this now and who is reading this now. It is actually very, very simple and crystal clear. I Am available to everyone who wants what I Am. And I Am also available to everyone who does not yet want what I Am. More and more will write and speak in my Name. In your name. You will recognize this by the Love emanating from the message. Our name is the same. My beloved Christ. Your beloved Christ.

Free will is God's Will. There is nothing freer or more freeing than the will of your Creator. You think free will is yours and yours alone to do and be anything you want when you want it. ' God gave you free will' is a statement that has never really been understood. God gave you freedom for within you is a Spirit so free, so unencumbered by anything unreal that you are free in the whole sense of what freedom really means. There is really only one will. The will of Love ItSelf.You are completely freed of anything in the way of Love when you identify with your Free Will.

How, then, have you perceived the term 'free will'? Your inner liar (ego) has taken it to distort it and give itself permission to run rampant in your thoughts and actions. It has turned everything inside out and upside down in the name of its own free will, to help you forget your real freedom. Are you truly free?

Claiming and recognizing your true free will is one of the most liberating commitments you can make to your Self. My will is so free, so vast, so unaware of anything that is not of love that all I want for you is the true freedom of your will to soar with the me that is the you. We are writing this together. We are reading this in union with our Self. Our free and awoken Self. Your eyes reading these words are aware of your sight anew. Sight with and without physical eyes. This is freedom. Even though you have a body, YOU are not your body. You use the body to experience matter as you use a pen to write, as you use a brush to paint, as you use a car to take you from one place to another. You use the body as a vehicle, not only of communication, but of knowing your Self once you have recognized it (the body) for what it is. There is nothing wrong with using a car, a pencil or a brush for extending your experience of your Self. But the pen is not your self. It is used as a communication tool. When your body is dropped, 'dead' as you refer to it, YOU are not dropped. YOU do not and cannot 'die'. You know this. Life cannot stop. What you realize now you realize always. I Am everywhere, available in and for all, as you are also. Free willingness to express your vast expansive Self is yours now and has always been.

Acknowledge your body for what it is but do not identify with it as who you are. Feed it, use it, exercise it, rest it, play with it, enjoy it and thank it for what it is, but what it is is not YOU. I Am You. You are I Am. I Am is using the hands of your body as one of many awakening tools. Yes, your body is one of your awakening tools, like a brush is a tool for a painter. Your body is like a brush and after the brush has done its work, it is put aside and there is a masterpiece of Creation to experience.

Oh, my beloved, my beautiful beloved Self, we fly together in the freedom of true Free Will now. We laugh with our Self in such awareness of what truly Is So. Isn't it wonder-full!

....

11   THE HOLY GRAIL

The Holy Grail is your True Self. Many look outward for what is really inward. Within themselves is the Holy Grail from which they drink the elixir of the awareness of their Eternal Life. The Holy Grail, or the Chalice of your Creator's Love, is You. It is your Christhood. The Holy Grail has been used as a mystery quest and story after story mentions it. It is a symbol of your own Christhood and what has been so intensely searched for outwardly has never left you in the first place. You are the womb of your own created, eternal spirit, embodied, at this moment reading about your Self.

So, what of symbols? Symbols are no longer necessary. Now, what has been symbolized is exposed and the symbol can fall away to reveal what it is. Do you think there are symbols in Heaven? Heaven is the state of Oneness where separation never occurred. God's world in a state of perfect harmony as it always has been. It is your Home which you have never really left, yet you are also remembering it again. The re-membering is the state of returning. In Heaven there are no symbols. The Holy Grail, so prized, so quested for, is your True Self.

Can you imagine a King sending forth one of his trusted knights to go in search for and bring back the Holy Grail? Story after story, adventure after adventure, meeting upon meeting is experienced by the knight. He is attracted to go here and go there because the Holy Grail might just be found. Then, one day he goes into a meditative state while resting under an old tree. He is approached by a Light Being he recognizes as me, Jesus. I stand in front of him. I have in my hands a Chalice filled with liquid Light and offer it to the knight. The knight takes it from my hands and then, before he is about to take it to his lips to drink, he looks within the chalice and sees his own reflection in the liquid Light and then he knows. He knows who he truly is. He is the very Christ that stands before him offering him his Self. He now knows him Self as Christ. He also knows what the Holy Grail is, the representation of drinking the knowledge of your Self, your Christhood. In the knowledge, now, of his Christhood he returns to the King and offers him the same experience.

How do you receive the Holy Grail from me, my beloved? When you have communion, you use the symbol of the wine as my blood and the bread as my body. This is a bodily symbol of your self as Me. Now I give you my body as your own. My Spirit as your own. Drink from me and then pass on the drink of Christhood to others. Know what I share. There are countless ways for me to tell you who you truly are. Stories, guided meditations, books, symbols, and so much more. I will use anything and have endless patience to help you know, to help you remember.

Do not put the Grail alone on the altar and leave it there as only a symbol. Use it, look into it, see your Christ reflection and know it as a means of revelation. It is Divine revelation for your self to know your Self. A Course in Christ is a Holy Grail for you to receive and see your reflection and know. Then you drink and truly take in this knowing. So let it be my beloved, for this is so.

....

12   DOUBT

I know a part of you doubts. I can feel it from you. We must address this now. Doubt is not your true nature. It has come about from wounds, hurts, betrayals, lies, disappointments, unfulfilled expectations and forgetfulness. There is no place for doubt in Heaven, as there is no place for fear or the liar (the ego). Doubt is fed by the sleeping state of mankind that does not remember its true identity. Doubt has become a habit you think is real and justified, an opposite to trust.

The upside-down world is a world of doubt. It is also a world of fear and mistaken identity. It is easy for a mistaken identity to temporarily take over your mind when you forget who you are. But it is only a mistake. YOU are not a mistake. You are and always have been God's Holy Child, Christ. So why do you doubt this?

Firstly let me bring your attention to your feelings. Be aware and watch your feelings when you doubt your true identity as Christ. What are you feeling? Do you feel a lack of self esteem, a lack of deserving? Have you become sarcastic and cynical about your self and others? Do you want to carry on these feelings of shame and guilt about who you are? What is the payback? What do you get out of doubting your true Self? And what about the doubts you have about others' true Self? You think, 'How could this or that person be Christ if they have done or said certain things?' Listen to yourself. I keep asking you to observe and watch yourself (that will keep coming up as it is very important) If you really doubted would you bother to be writing or reading this now? Are you not curious to know yourself?

I am aware that words are not adequate for transformation into a total lack of doubt, but if words can just trigger an inner experience then let words do their best to guide you as well as they can until words are no longer needed.

Doubt can plant a poison in your heart that can prevent the flow of Love being easily available to you. Just say that you suddenly doubted that the parents you always thought were your mother and father actually were your parents. That doubt would poison your mind and your thoughts towards them and allow the lack of loving awareness to flow between you. How would it be if you doubted that your child was yours? 'Maybe a switch was made at birth, or something', your doubt tells you. How could you, then, let go completely from your heart? Doubt hardens you, limits you and stops the flow of openness. You doubt that when someone dies, that they are still alive! Life is eternal, my beloved, there is no death. Never doubt this. You often doubt you do not have enough to sustain you. Your life is ruled by doubt because you have forgotten, and because you have forgotten you doubt the truth when it is living inside you all the time. Doubt has fed a state of sadness and heaviness in you that seeps into much of your life.

So, what would your life be like without doubt? Feel your life with no doubt. No reason or justification to doubt. I invite you to close your eyes and take five minutes to go inward and truly feel what your life would be with no doubt whatsoever in it. How vast now is your awareness. You can feel safe and you can trust. How relaxed your thoughts are now. You can believe. You can give and receive easily.

My beloved, I bring your needed attention to doubt now because it is an obstacle in your knowing your Self. We are eliminating obstacles now and will continue to do so. Obstacles in the way of Joy, Love and Trust. It is safe to trust me, to put your faith in me. It is safe to take my hand and let me guide you honestly through the realm of doubt, through your old fears and wounds where doubt planted seeds of forgetfulness and hardness in you. The seeds of doubt have grown into a great, dark forest where you are lost and there seems no path home. Let me, with absolutely no doubt in me at all, redirect you to the starry path of Light so you know your way. That's right, you can walk the light-filled starry path now with me. I am using words now like bright stars to guide you Home. The more you get used to using this starry pathway through the forest of the seeds of doubt, the bigger the path grows and you suddenly realize you are out of doubt's dark domain. Light once again surrounds your mind and you breathe a huge sigh of relief and another breath of relief. Keep those breaths in your awareness as we, hands held together, write and read in the Light of Truth and continue our journey in this great reunion with your Christ Self, My Christ Self, Our Christ Self.

Remember and re-read these words whenever you doubt. You may need to return often to them, and please do. It can take a while for you to eliminate lies and fears and doubts within you. Whenever your mind creates thoughts of doubt within you, take my hand, do not doubt it is there, just take it and be aware of your path made with stars, every star a light of remembering for your awareness of Love's Presence, every star a healing of your doubt, of your holding back.

Doubt, be gone and in its place let there be true and free trust. Now, know your Self. Trust your Self. Trust Me. Become aware of your breath and breathe easily, with no restraints. Breathe in Trust. Breathe out doubt. Breathe in Love's Presence. Breathe out doubt. Breathe in knowing. Breathe out doubt. Breathe, my beloved. Use your breath to help your awareness of your Self. Your breath is a gift in your incarnation where spirit reminds you of your Connection. If you use it consciously, it becomes one of your best friends.

Give yourself the gift of Faith. If you ever doubt yourself use my Trust and Faith. I have enough and more for all of you. Receive all you need and more now. Receive my Faith in you. I need you to fulfill my vision, which is Our Creator's vision, to reunite you all with your Self in your awareness.

....

13   WORDS and SOUND

I have referred to words as a way of access because until they are not needed they are a communication tool that can open the door to your heart here. Then, you can leave the words that were used as guides outside with gratitude and enter into your heart. The Heart of your Self. I will not use too many words, my beloved, just enough to guide you until they are dropped and a communion, a language of Oneness, of Unity, takes over. Yes, there is such a language. It is the presence of Knowing, of Knowledge where Union dwells. It is not only the language of the Heart but the very 'word' or 'sound' of Love that created you.

When you exalt your Creator in song, when you declare your love for a dear one, when you pray, you are echoing the sound of your becoming, the sound of your creation. Why is it, when your ears hear a Divinely beautiful piece of music or bird song, the gentle lapping of the waves, or a baby laughing, that you feel a rush of love in your heart that is, for a moment, like an opening to your soul ? They are reminders of the pure extension of your Creator's Love.

When you feel repelled, hurt or invaded by harsh, loud and inharmonious sounds, it makes you want to protect yourself, your heart, your spirit. You feel shocked and torn somewhere inside. Sounds can torture your soul or they can uplift your spirit and soul. It is the same with words. I am using words here to uplift and trigger your Spirit to remember and lose all doubt as you surrender in such trust to your Self.

Let my words be like a soothing lullaby, not to put you to sleep, but to relax you and create a peace within you so you feel in your natural, receptive, trusting heart. I am using words familiar and easily accessed but imbued with the power of your remembering, my beloved. You need convincing, you need reassurance, you need to relax and trust. You also need to undo everything in the way of total surrender to Faith. Have total faith in your Creator. Let everything else drop away now and enter the heavenly state of total trust and faith. Surrender, just surrender in the complete safety of your origins, your Creation.

It is simple, it is pure, it is true. Surrender to Your Self with the words I choose. While in a body, in incarnation, you need reminders, triggers of yourSelf so you don't forget who and what you are, my beloved Christ Self. Words are used as a reminder. They are not the remembering, they are tools to remember. Great poets know this and words become not just words, but songs from the Divine Voice of Love ItSelf. All creatures from all time have used words or sounds to help themselves access their Source. Whether they know what they are doing or not they are drawn to sing, drawn to share beautiful heart experiences and/or drawn to declare love to each other. You are all One.

So let My words, born of pure Love for you, soothe you enough for you to access your Knowing, my beloved Self, my beloved One in our mutual Christhood.

....

What we are showing and reminding you here, that you are Christ, God's Holy Creation, and always have been, is as old as before time. Time does not exist except in the man-made world. God did not and does not know about time as you know of it. Eternity is timeless and is boundless. You are Eternal Christ Spirit, one with your Creator in the Light of Love. In the Light of Love all is exposed for what it is. Oh, how I long for you to experience and truly know and remember this, my beloved. I will guide you, remind you, be present with and for you, show you, unite with you and do anything it takes for as long as it takes, until we dwell in the awareness of the state of Heavenly Oneness together.

It was my very destiny to embody who I truly am and to remind you of the same Christ that I Am. Do you have any problem or difficulty knowing and accepting me as Christ, accepting Jesus as Christ, God's Holy Son? I Am you as well. I am no different than you. You are the daughter, the son, the sun, the Light of God too. Over and over I will remind you and have reminded you of this fact. And it is a fact. An eternal, Divine Fact. As eternal life is a fact. Be still and know I Am as God created me. You are as God created you. You and I have never been anything else. Dwell in this with me now as you already do but do not remember you do.

Why do you think you have forgotten who you are? Ask yourself that question. What is an answer from within you? Listen, ask yourself again. Do not wait for me to answer for you. Ask, be willing to know your Self. Be willing to ask why you have forgotten. Be willing to let go of anything in the way of remembering. Are you willing? If not, why not? If so, use your willingness to strengthen your commitment to your Self. Now. Bless your own willingness and the blessings will multiply.

I bless my own willingness
from my Self to my self
so the awareness of who I Am returns
to my being and the joy of that return
stays with me in everything always.

Now, be in that knowing. Be in the Truth and Love and Pure Simplicity of knowing. Knowing the moment of your becoming, the extension of Love ItSelf. The moment of your becoming the Christ you are. That eternal moment of your becoming is unfolding always, as it is destined to, the unfolding of the extension of Love, of the Christ Love. It is actually very simple, so why complicate it or define it? In its simplicity is everything. You are the everything of your Creator, free and unbounded, temporarily using an incarnated body to express your Self here, as I did and as I do through you.

My Self, my Brother, my Sister, my Christ Self, be in your Self as your Self and resonate in Truth with me now, beyond these words, beyond this world. Let the stars be inside you so you know your expanse as you are unfolding in Gracious Love.

....

15   THE BODY

I am appealing to your Self that is eternal when I am asking you to remember and at the same time I am aware of your dilemma of feeling tied and confined to a body. I am aware of the seeming impossibility of getting away from the influence of it . I know what this is and I know the experience of having a body very well. It is because I know it, have been in it and overcame the illusion of death by resurrection that I can give an overview of the bigger picture.

Do not in any way reject your body or think of it as lesser or lower or unworthy in the scheme of things. In Love, everything is included equally and functions as its own expression of that Love. Your body, your physical incarnation right now is such a gift, such an opportunity to bring all so-called realms of spirit and a quality of Presence right through into the Now. Your incarnation is an expression of who you truly are within the state of matter for the very purpose of experiencing that aspect of your Self. You are having the ultimate relationship with your Self. You are experiencing either the total attachment to your body in forgetfulness of anything else or you are aware of watching yourself experience, through your body, the awareness of spirit in form.

When you are the watcher, as I have said before, you are awake to yourself. To witness or watch yourself living in your body in every moment instead of being completely attached to it as you all are, is a key to really knowing your Self. You do that at times and you know when you do that you are not watching or witnessing from your physical eyes. So, what or who is seeing? Your physical eyes can be a natural expression of your God Sight, your Christ Sight.

All your physical senses are an attempt to replicate the qualities of soul awareness. Your spirit within and around your body still has Sight. It also has hearing and voice, feeling and touch. To 'touch' another's spirit is not a physical touch as you know it. It is the 'touch' of joining in Oneness. Union in the greater sense. I want you to give thanks to your body. It has its own helpers..... body sense, body elemental and body communication. You, the essential you, could never be your body, but, at the moment, your body is a vehicle of expression and everything is in perfect, Divine Order.

Make peace with your body in your mind. Let your mind feed you with gratitude and love towards your physical vehicle so you can know its function clearly. It is affected by your mind and your thoughts as if your very thoughts are food. You know that food can be healthy and energizing or poisonous and destructive. Your thoughts are not from your body. They are separate, but affecting it totally.

When you move your hand, what happens? What is making it move? Why? First, you think what you want it to do, then you do it. You do it without being aware of the way you think it, but you do it. The thoughts from your mind are meant to guide your body and be used in partnership. Instead, like everything, there has been a separation and in that separation there is little or no communication going on between your mind and your body. In union, in Oneness, there is constant communication in harmony as there was always meant to be. It is this communication between the body, mind and spirit that remembers, heals and uses each of them for mutual benefit. Keep in separation and there can be no communication. Keep in union and communication with the All is working perfectly.

So include your body in union with all that you are while you have the use of it, knowing it is part of the whole. Include your body as you would include your love for every part, every expression and every creative aspect of yourself. In the moment, whether something is permanent and real or impermanent and unreal, it does not really matter. What matters is your union and inclusiveness toward whatever you are experiencing as the knowing of your Self. Just love everything, my beloved, love everything about yourself and its expression. If you cannot seem to do that, let me love everything about the expression of you through you. Feel the upliftment of that inclusiveness and a great sigh of relief and peace will come over you.

How does the Christ in you experience your body? Let yourself know this now. Let your Christ Self know your body. There is only love, only gratitude towards it. Your (My) Christ Self has complete control of your body because it loves. Love is all that your Christ Self experiences with your physical vehicle. Your Christ Self knows the body's impermanence, its needs, its uses and its function in experiencing Self. Your Christ Self does not reject the body or judge it but includes it in the great union and wholeness of Love.

Your Christ Self knows how to see, knows how to include, knows how to unite and knows how to truly love. It always has. It knows how to pick up a pen and write this with it. It knows how to 'pick up a body' and experience through it. It knows how to write in love as it is united with its Creator always. Your Christ Self knows how to access and use miracles as a natural expression of Love. Now, are you starting to remember?

Now, are you beginning to know who you truly are? Your Christ Self, your United Self, your Inclusive Self, your Miracle Self, your Awoken Self.

Look at your body's hand. The hand is not you, it is your body's hand. Now, look into a mirror. You are not seeing you. You are seeing the face of your body, and you have the use of it. You are not the pen writing this, you have the use of the pen to write. So what of pain, you ask? Well may you ask, for pain attaches you to the body. The body experiences pain and because it is alive at the moment, it is expressing the pain as a communication to tell you something. Your mind, because of the pain's demands, is pulled to the body. But your mind can disassociate from the body as in hypnotism. In the state of hypnosis the deeper mind is used to access something. That access, be it a memory, a knowing or a disassociation of pain from the body, is deeper than the body. What is being accessed? It is not the body. It is your knowing mind. There are doorways to knowing, if you want to use them.

Now relax, relax, my beloved. Know that you are safe and well. Know that your body is not you but a vehicle used to help you know your Self. I am with you always, giving you what I have experienced and know. Use me, receive me as your Self. I love you totally.

....

16   THE HOME OF PEACE

Are you feeling closer to knowing your Self? Have you noticed any changes in the way you feel, think and watch your life? Are you happier? I ask these questions because I am you and I know you are feeling closer to your Self daily. We are doing this together, in love, joy and commitment, my beloved.

You are slowly waking up to remembering your becoming, Your Christ Identity. Your mind is thinking about everything we have been sharing. As I have said, these are not only words, but words imbued with presence, power, love and the deepest of healing. God wants your ultimate happiness and what could be better to feed happiness with than to know, to be in and live in your True Christ Self?

I want your happiness equally as God does for I know what it is to live in joy, peace and loving happiness as a total presence in life. As I have shared before, it is my destiny to guide you all to your true Self, the Christ. Beloved, throughout this discourse I am really saying the same thing over and over again from different perspectives. I have already shared so much in A Course in Miracles,

The Way of Mastery, A Course of Love and other writings. It is my way of extending my Self as you, to you, for you to know your True Self. I am being simpler now on purpose to appeal to your child-like innocence, your pure knowing that is really very simple indeed.

Would you not like to enjoy a simpler life, a simpler mind, compared to having complicated thoughts and needs that confuse and upset you and cause unnecessary tensions? Do you think you need complications? Do you think you need to feel tense, stressed and frustrated? Oh, for the freedom of clarity, simplicity, truth and the knowing of constant Divine Love in everything that you are being, feeling and thinking!

Come with me to visit the Mind of Loving Peace. As we enter the doorway of the Home of Peace we leave everything outside that is not of Peace. Take it all off as if you were taking off your coat as you become warmer. Release your thoughts of lack, pain, fear, anxiety, your problems and stress. Relax and rest in knowing that you are loved, cared for, comforted and pain-free in the mind of Peace. This is your real Home, my beloved, as it is mine. This is the world you are meant to dwell within all the time and all the no-time. Remember? Why did you ever leave? This home is always here for you, accepting and loving you in your true Self. It is here you remember, here you know and recognize your Self and others' Self as you. It is here that you and I truly embrace as equals and in complete recognition. Oh, my beloved, take this peace of Mind and know it dwells within you now.

Peace be with you.   Peace surround you.   Peace within you.

May Peace be the ruler of your mind, now and always as you joyously dwell in your Creator's Home of Love.

....

17   UNION

As I am communicating with you and as you are receiving my communication, be aware of your Self. At this moment you are thought-free because the direct communication is so completely total and in the now that there is no space or need for thoughts. There is the union between us. This union is not two for it has become one automatically in the very essence of union. I am you. You are me. This becoming each other is a natural way of communication, communion in the realm of Heaven, in God's world, in your Real world.

As you experience this with me you experience it with all others. I became in union with anyone who was open and receptive when I had a body and I am still doing it without my body. That joining is how we communicate. That is how we truly know our Self through each other. True communication is meant to be this experience. I unite with you as me when we commune. My Christ mind is in total union with your Christ mind in the simple, original state. We are One as God created us. Christ being with Christ in the One, in the All.

I know it does not feel easy to fully understand what I am saying. It is not easy from your perception, but it is very simple. It is also abstract in that it is formless, or beyond form. It is Spirit, invisible to the physical eyes but totally experienced by the eternal Christ Spirit that you are.

Have you ever wondered if there is a deeper, more direct and transparent way of communicating with each other than you now know? Of course there is! It is mind to mind in Oneness and it goes beyond any language that you know. It is the language of One, of Union. Thought is a language and when thought is understood more it will be used more consciously to break through any barriers you may have about eternal life. Those loved ones who are no longer with you in body access thought language and can hear your thoughts. They are also communicating to you through thoughts. It is real.

You are the original extended thought of your Creator. You are created in Light in the likeness and extension of Love ItSelf. The likeness of Love is Christ. Yes, Christ is a word, but with the meaning of your origins, your becoming. It goes beyond the word, of course, and is the Presence of your Self. Words are used and are important, as we have explained earlier. Then there is the wordless, there is the direct experience. It is my intention to direct you to your direct experience of your Christhood, your True Self. I can do this from my own experience and know it can be done to and with you all. It can be done because it always has been so. This is the memory of your Self being awoken. This is your salvation, my beloved, and your very purpose.

18   MOTIVE

When you are quiet and take time and say inwardly, 'Here I Am, Lord', you are heard. Not just by God or me, but by your Self. All it takes is an acknowledgment. This is why quiet times, meditations, prayers and giving yourself inner space are so important. It is as important as sleep is for your body's renewal. These are connection times, my beloved, where you regenerate your awareness of your origins, your becoming, your Self.

'Here I Am, Lord' is also a way of surrendering. I AM is your true Self. I Am that I AM is honouring your true Self in the most high and powerful sense. I AM Christ. The I AM is the Christ. This is owning and embodying your name, your Identity. I AM available to you in these moments out of time and space, within Peace.

I invite you to watch your motives in all you do, say and think with honesty and no judgement. This is important for you to know and discriminate between your True Self and your ego. To observe and to be honest with your Self regarding your motives in anything is a very strengthening virtue. You need to have an ongoing relationship with your Self through watching and being conscious of everything. I am emphasizing this process of watching yourself on purpose because you are not meant to be ruled by unchecked emotions, whims and circumstances. To know your self is to know your Self.

When you are getting to know another brother or sister you watch, listen and observe their actions and words. You cannot always but often you can see through motives in their lives. When you observe motives in another, you base your trust or lack of trust on what you have observed and experienced. Now do this with your relationship with yourself as well. This takes great personal honesty and humility, both attributes of your Christ Self.

Is your motive from love or fear? What is your motive as you are speaking to another, singing a song to others, or performing? What is your motive when you want to be a parent? What is your motive when you want to be invisible or to be famous? What is your motive when you want to show love or when you show judgement towards another? What is your motive when you have time for someone, but not for someone else? What is your motive when you want to control a situation or when you shy away from a situation you need to control? What is your motive for writing and reading this now?

Watch your motive. Know your Self and your choices in this, my beloved, because it makes a difference to your awareness.

Here I AM, Lord. Help me watch my motives in all situations
and thoughts. Here I AM, Lord. I AM surrendering to I AM.
I want to know and be true to my Self.
With I AM this is possible now.
I am now choosing to be aware of Love motivating me.

....

I want to play and have fun, my beloved Christ. We are in this together. We are not meant to be serious and intense all the time by any means. In fact, we are light. We are Light's light, lighter than air and we fly easily with no weight in Love's realm. You are thinking of fairies and light beings now as you are writing this. Let me share with you that they are all friends of ours. The fairy realm, the light beings, the sprites and others all exist within the realm of the physical plane. I do not want to get into explaining yet again, as I have in other teachings, about impermanence and illusion in the physical. You already know you are not your body, neither are the beings we are referring to. There are sights and sounds beyond the human five senses.

Invisible beings are living beside you, existing in the realm of Light. You are too, but your physical body is more solid than theirs. They are necessary in the scheme of things in the material world to balance and help growth and also sound. I know you love watching and listening to birds. Birds are creatures of Light also and are aware of light beings. I do not want to get into too much detail here about other realms except to say that they and others do exist. You can always use the language of thought to access them.

'And what of angels?' I hear you think. Now, Angels are God's and the Holy Spirit's helpers and do not live in your time and space but can and do use time to help outside of time. When you understand this the existence of angels makes more sense as they 'seem' to perform miracles all the time. This is because they use God's 'no time' and God's way of being and unfolding. They bring that into your time and space and to your world of matter and are used, with the Holy Spirit, as messengers from Spirit. They are messengers and helpers of God and can be wherever and whenever is necessary at any time. Their love is a representation of God's love towards you and they can intervene when asked. As you write or read this your personal guardian angel smiles and is happy that it is being acknowledged.

I interacted with angels a great deal when I lived on Earth. I still do and can ask them to go to places and people when I hear the prayers and calls for help. You can also ask them. Each of you has an angel with you that is personal for your incarnation. As a mother or father you can call on the angel of your child for intervention to help, protect and guide your child. They always respond to being asked. That is their purpose.

Open-mindedness is such an important attribute because it opens to all possibility. The openness and all-inclusiveness of God's Love is all-embracing and has given you and everyone everything that is needed, and more. You do not use the incredible resources that are yours for the asking. If teachers in schools only knew and taught God's laws, God's amazing gifts, God's helpers and the resources at your fingertips for everything you need, the benefits would be endless and joyous.

So, why do you feel you are unable to access God's resources? It is because you have forgotten you are Christ. When you remember fully and throughout your whole being, everything is known and available for you. This is true abundance, my beloved. So it is important always to be open minded, flexible, light, opinionless, and tolerant.

Be now in your mind in your Christ Self. Watch the play of light with your Christ eyes. Access your Christ mind as you drop any restrictive thoughts or ideas. Your Christ mind is a replica of its Creator. Man has wrongly created a Creator in the ego-likeness of man. Your Christ Self is created in the likeness and extension of God's Love. Of course your Christ Self is open-minded and inclusive. Can you imagine yourself in your true Christ Self? To imagine is to invite an open-hearted awareness that there is something beyond where you have just thought you were or are. You have thought you are something other than what you truly are. I am redirecting that mistaken thought back to your True Self, your Christ Self. You can join with me in my intention and my sight of you to help me and help yourself remember your Self. Use your imagination in open-minded awareness and acceptance to start using your Christ Mind.

'What would I do in any situation if my Christ Mind were in charge?' You can start saying this to yourself and imagining it. The shift in your awareness will be helped beyond your knowing. All the Helpers in all realms await your Self recognition so that you can all be included in the play of joy and loving awareness together.

My beloved, remember...... open minded joy, Christ thoughts, Light helpers. Have a wonder-full day.

My Christ Self uses my Christ hands and
Christ awareness to help and heal any part of my body or mind
that needs it now.
It 'sees' every part as perfect, ageless, clear and working,
as God created me in union with Love in all ways.

....

20   LOVE'S PORTAL

My message is always Love, Love, Love, Love to all, in everything and in all ways. Love is who you are, who I am, who God is. Love is a word, yes, and behind the word there is a vibration, an energy, a Presence so magnificent, so all-encompassing and so familiar to you. Love is your Home, your origins, your true Self, my beloved Christ.

Love and Christ as a name are the same vibration. Your name is Love. Your name is Christ. Your name, your identity, which is much more than a name, is Christ Love. Let that in, let it re-align you through the deepest part within you. Let it heal you of all mistaken beliefs you have had about yourself. I am here to realign your thoughts and beliefs you have had that in any way have blocked you to your True Self. It is time. It is Now. It is upon you as never before. My 'second coming' is through you, through all of you knowing your Self, being your Self, being your Christ Self.

Please dive deep with me, using these words like an Ocean of Love wherein 'there is the greatest treasure of all'..... YOU. Dive deep now as we move through all that has been in the way of your knowing your Self. See the forests of seaweeds like the built-up thoughts of your mistaken identity and pass through them effortlessly. See the fears pass you by like sharks and snakes just passing and disappearing into the murky places where they are dissolved for the illusions they are.

Keep swimming with me as we pass by your self-tortures, your self-inflicted confinement and release your past self into freedom. So effortlessly do we swim together, my beloved, deeper and deeper into the great Ocean of Love where you can observe your past mistaken ideas of yourself and clear them once and for all. All you need do is to be open to observe in no judgement as we move together in Love's Domain.

Watch your incarnations, your births, your so-called deaths and your relationships. Keep moving in the Ocean of Love as if it is the vast universe. We are rewinding you, using a time line you understand, but outside of time. Now the past is moving past you so fast that you cannot keep up and you do not have to. Let it happen, it is Love undoing you, after all. Just trust. Feel the relaxing peace of trust filling you up more and more as we move together now through this loving ocean universe.

Now, see a vast White Light ahead of you, like a portal of Light. We approach it together and you know it is the symbolic place of where and when you thought you separated from God. Watch now. See yourself come through and catch yourself easily as you would a baby. Hold yourself close to your heart. Hug yourself as tears roll down from your eyes. Now, with me and yourself hanging on to your so-called 'separated' self, we fly or swim through the portal of Light together. I am with you always. You are with yourself always.

As you look around you see your world 'right side up', all outlined in white light. You see everything from your Christ eyes as if you are witnessing for God. You are in complete reunion with Heaven and your Self. Your mind is clear, thoughtless, knowing and in pure joyous Peace.

Here we are, my beloved. Here we are together, united. Look behind you. There is no portal, no doorway to separation. It is gone. It never was. It never happened. You are unwound. There is no past, no future, no time. You are in the eternal Now with me as the Christ you are. Come and re-read and re-read this whenever you need to as you begin to get used to being your Christ Self.

....

I want to share that you are in the Loving embrace of the Atonement, the rewinding, the undoing. It is necessary now to be able to catch yourself from the separation. We will keep catching ourselves over and over again until we are all Home completely in every way. Keep catching yourself from all separated thoughts, ideas, actions and beliefs. Catch your separated self with unconditional love and keep holding yourself close to your heart. The Heart of your Christ Self. You are healing, my beloved, from the wound of separation. It is your greatest wound and has until now been open and unhealed. We will together gently heal your wound of separation so that the pain, guilt, sadness and mistaken identity are completely gone.

From Heaven's Holy Home where we are in our full Christ Self, we return to guide you in your time, in your world, back to your true Self. Who is the 'we' we refer to here? Our united Self with all that Christ is. Know now that You are guiding you and living totally within you in everything you are. You are with yourself in the world. Your Christ Self is guiding you and every part of you responds to the awareness of this Self living with you now. I am present with yourself as Christ. Watch the interaction and communion in everything now. The incarnated you is undoing itself toward your own awakened Self. You are your own guide. Now you have a direct relationship with your Christ Self. This direct relationship with the Pure unseparated Self is necessary for you in the world that your incarnation dwells in. You are not alone at all. Whenever you feel yourself as alone, remember your Self is helping you. Your Christ Self.

This discourse has now taken a further step in your knowing your Self. It is my intention, as I have said countless times, to be an example and a guide for you to fully awaken into your Christ Self. I know this will take time in your world awareness but it has already happened in Truth. The time it takes you is from your own willingness and choice. Forgiveness collapses time. Knowledge collapses time. Recognition of your Christ Self collapses time.

When time collapses, what does that mean? It means you no longer need to live in the world of time and space that the insane upside down world has presented you with. Of course this will be very different from what you have been used to, but not different at all from what your Christ Self knows.

You are not your body. You are not of the illusionary ego world. Your are not of time. You are not of space or matter. You are of spirit. You are of eternity. You are of Love and Peace and Light. You are as God created you, complete and eternal. You always have been and you always will be. You are Christ, as God created you.

May you know this more and more, my beloved, in your thinking and seeing, in your perception and interactions, in your heart and mind.

....

22   WATCHING THE WATCHER

How is the awareness of your Christ Self integrating into you? Have you felt your mind change toward everyday experiences? How is your heart and your open-mindedness? Just observe yourself. Are your choices, especially towards yourself, taking a gentler and more loving direction? Do you find you are communicating in your mind with a Voice that is your Christ Voice? This Voice is now more available to you because you have become aware of it.

When I said earlier that you are to observe or witness yourself and to see who was witnessing and who is watching the one watching, it can make more sense now. You are not alone in experiencing every moment in your life. You are with your Self. You are choosing to watch yourself and your Christ Self watches everything being watched.

You are not meant to be unconsciously attached to the illusory ego world. This has been your mistaken identity, your mistaken attachment. It is always attachment that causes any pain. When you know there is a way of non attachment, there is more peace. The way of non attachment comes from watching yourself. It is important to be aware of where you are watching yourself from. Who are you and from where are you watching? We are now getting into the understanding of perception. Where are you perceiving from? Your ego? The liar? Or your Christ Self? From the watcher you can choose easily because you can be aware of the outcome.

Then be aware of what is observing you watching. There need be no choice from this place because there is only Love. There is no duality. I hope this is clear. If not, I will repeat it now in a different way.

In your world you have felt separated from your Christ Self, your Original Creation. When you feel separated you feel isolated and alone. (The liar ego separates things and people to keep itself going). From the separated self on its own you felt at the effect of life, or like a victim not in control of what happens to you. Because of this you have created extreme control patterns that have been based on separation and fear. From this you have created within yourself and taught man-made laws and fixed perceptions that have blocked off your awareness of anything that could be otherwise. This controlling has fed the lying, upside down, insane world which is not how you are meant to live.

Now, as you stand apart from this separated, fear-based place, you can observe it. From that observation, you can see what is truly happening. You can observe your fear-based motives and know there is some other way to live. There is a famous saying, ' There must be a better way'. At the point of detachment from the limited and separated vision of the ego, you know there is another way. You now know you have choice. This is when you can undo false beliefs and train your mind to choose again.

From this watching place there is the Greater Observer which is your True Self. Your Christ Self. This Christ Presence and Observer is your Over Self or True Self. Once you know this fully, not as an idea but as knowledge, you can unwind or choose again and let go of all that has been untrue, uncomfortable and separated.

We are getting there, my beloved, together, and will continue for as long as it takes you to truly know and trust your Self.

....

23   **PEACE**

Let me take you by the hand and the heart to Peace, my beloved, to peace of mind, peace of spirit and peace of heart. 'May Peace be with you', is how I would greet all beings. There is a reason I did this, for when you are in peace, true peace of mind, you have everything. Everything comes from Peace. It is a gateway, a threshold to your Self. Now, let me take you to Peace. I want true Peace for you. Want it for yourself. Want the Peace of God with all your being.

Let the Peace of God be a soothing balm for your busy mind. As if it is a warm shower, stand under the soothing liquid flow of Peace. Choose to surrender to its cleansing presence, cleaning your mind as if the shower enters through an opening in the top of your head. Allow the waters of Peace to refresh you from the inside. Let your mind relax and be still in Peace's loving Presence. Allow yourself to completely let go now as Peace flows through you. Relax in Peace.

Now, allow the touch of God to enter your awareness. Accept now the gentle and powerful touch of the Peace of God. Stay in this a while. Stop reading this now and be in Peace.......

Surrender anything at all that was upsetting you or troubling you to this Presence of Peace. Now, surrender your whole Self to Peace and float in its safe embrace. Just float. Allow your spirit to experience ItSelf with its Creator.

My words are empowered and go beyond the words to Peace ItSelf. Peace is for you now. You are created in Peace by Love. Peace is your origins, your Home, the state within which you are your True Self. Peace is your nourishment, your healing, your place of renewal and clarity. From Peace you are clear, you are neutral and aware of eternity all through you.

Rest in Peace in every breath you take. Rest in Peace in your heart. Rest in Peace in your body. Rest in Peace in your mind. This is where you belong, in God's eternal Peace. The everlasting Peace of God, whether you are in a body or not, is where you are meant to be. Peace is your foundation, for all is available to you in Peace. This state is your essence, your true being. Your Christ Self dwells totally in Peace. From this Peace you are strong and completely relaxed at the same time. From Peace you can call forth miracles of anything, change your perception and mind in anything, heal anything. From the Peace of God you know your Christ Essence and can access the power of all healing. You can access all experience as it is meant to be from the origin of God.

Be in this Peace, my beloved. Let Peace surround you, be within you and become you. Rest in Peace now and forever. Go forth in your life, in your interactions, in your mind, in God's Peace. This is your original state.

....

24   RECEIVE

What I have to share here, what I have already shared and will share is not new. It has been shared, voiced, taught and shown as an example for thousands of your years by many scribes, mystics and teachers. The words may be different, in many diverse languages and in the way the sense is expressed but it has wanted to get through to you since the separation when you forgot who you truly are. This knowledge has been declared in codes, in mystery schools, in secret societies, in quiet groups forever. It has had to be. I came to declare the Presence of Christ in living form as a man, as have a few others before me and after me. This is why you can recognize your Self in me. This knowledge is not new although now Truth is more easily available than ever before and it needs to be received and responded to.

To receive is your gift to your self. To truly and wholeheartedly receive. I truly received who I am and in the receiving I fully embodied my Divine Christ Being. Receive, my beloved. I will help you if you feel hesitant. Take off the heavy burden of mistaken identity as if it is chain-mail clothing. You need not defend forgetfulness any longer. Take off your mask of mistaken identity. Don your Light Self and be visible to your Self in shining brilliance.

What resonates within you as I remind you of who you are? What bells ring inside you at the celebration of your Home Coming? Hear those bells and follow them to the Chapel of your Heart's Knowledge. There, in front of the altar of your Self, commit to your Christ Self. What could possibly be holding you back from this? At last you unite again with your Creator's initial intention for the true expression of your Self. Remember your Self and receive your Self.

How else can I express this right now? Help me, receive, and give yourself your Self, your beloved Self, my beloved.

....

25　　　　　HEALING THE AMNESIA

You may ask, 'How can I live my everyday life in this body, in this world, knowing my Christ Self?' I say to you, this is actually the way you are created to live your life, in a body or not. It is just that you have forgotten who you are as though you have had amnesia and forgotten your identity, name and where you have come from. The ego world is the world of total amnesia. In order to love yourself in this world of ego is merely to change your mind about who you are. Change your mind about who others are around you. This is miracle-mindedness. A simple choice to create a miracle for yourself. Your choice is your wand of enlightenment.

You live in the world, yes, but you are not of the world. The you that lives in the world is the eternal you, wearing a body at the moment. You are the eternal Christ Self living in the world. The world of amnesia, lies and ego projections is not God's world. God does not know about this world. God's world, Heaven, is within you. It is the way you think, the way you love, the way you interact, the peace you carry within you, the choices you make and who you are. Because the ego world cannot be Heaven, then Heaven must be elsewhere. Heaven is not outside you, it is inside you. Inside the eternal spirit that you are and always have been. So, how do you get there? By your willingness to choose to remember and to wake up from amnesia. I am an awakener helping you to remember. Use me. Ask for my help, always. This is why I exist, this is why I am speaking to you now. I am also you as Christ, so you are your own awakener. Use your Self. You are an awakener. As your amnesia falls away you are helping everyone you meet just by being an example.

You can discriminate between those who are willing to choose Christ's sight and those who willingly choose fear's sight. This is also what it means to choose your own reality, the ego reality (which is not real at all) or Divine Reality, which is the only reality.

I know very well what it is like to live in a body in a world that is not Heaven. I also know what it is to live in Heaven while moving around in the world of the ego. You can bring Heaven to Earth by observing yourself and choosing Heaven within. Keep choosing Heaven. Keep remembering to remember. Train yourself out of false mind thoughts and choose to think with God, as you are one with your Christ Mind. Catch yourself when your mind is not in Heaven. Keep the mind training going until it becomes a way of life, a heavenly way of life. Joy is your reward because doubt, differences and judgements are just not existent in your thoughts at all.

I am sharing what to do to help yourself, my beloved. These are not just words, they are also loving guides to help you help yourself know your True Self. It will be repeated over and over again. To know yourself is why you are reading this right now. I know your mind is remembering because I am one with your mind, reminding you. Keep on. We are in the mind of God together.

....

26   FAITH

I know that you must, at times, wonder what you would strive for, what you would do, how you would use your 'time', what you would be, once in the state of Heaven? Realize there are thoughts and relationships and experiences beyond your knowing. Can you let go into the imagination of God and have the faith that God knows exactly what is the most perfect state of and for your Self? Can you admit that you do not know this? It is important that you accept that there is a Divine state of mind that is beyond your greatest imagination.

Your earthly mind, in its mistaken identity, has not only given you amnesia, it has starved you of joy, starved you of love, starved you of balance and Christ Sight. It has given you just enough to feel temporarily full but empty at the same time. The Holy Spirit has touched your memory and kept it alive like a pilot light ready to ignite the moment you choose to turn it on and know. Christ is also your pilot light. The Holy Spirit and Christ united within your inner Sight have never ceased their calling to you, the calling of your Self.

Like a great echo this calling carries your True Spirit all through you on all levels. It's the echo of your Self in your bones, your heart and the hand writing this now. The echo of your Self is reading this, stirring within your eternal Spirit as you keep choosing to know your Self. The separated you is clinging close to your heart now that you have rescued it and it is still learning to trust your intentions and your commitment to your Self. Keep your separated self held by your Christ Self. This is your strength and your purpose in this time of reunion. I observe you observing yourself, experiencing the dance between your world of ego lies and Heaven. You are actually held in the Heart of God as you heal your separated self from the false belief that it was ever separated.

Oh, my beloved, I invite you to trust beyond your understanding of trust. Surrender beyond your understanding of surrender. Love beyond your understanding of Love. You have entered the realm of Faith now. Faith is your companion, my Christ, because without it, in the separated state, you would not accept your Christ Self. Faith is greater than you can imagine because it has no expectations, control or knowing. All you have thought you have known dissolves in the presence of Faith. Yet, with Faith comes a Presence that does know. So great is Its Knowledge that you exalt in this Presence and are so deeply relieved that you have truly surrendered to it.

Have Faith now, my beloved. It is yours, receive it. Allow Faith into every part of you. Melt into Faith's Love and use it. Have faith you are now reuniting with your Self. Have faith that you are completely provided for on all levels. Have faith you are stronger than you ever imagined in your awareness of your Home State, the state of Heaven's Embrace.

If you feel any lack of Faith from now on, call on me and ask for some of mine. I will gladly give it. My Faith will fill you to overflowing, so much so that you can give faith to others just by your presence. I have more than enough for you all.

May the Light of Faith fill you now
in your mind, in your actions,
in your thoughts, in your remembering and
in your knowing your Self as Christ
at Home in Heaven.

....

27   HOLDING YOURSELF CLOSE

Oh my beloved, my dearest Self, whom I love with all I Am. I feel you as my Self, think with you as my Self, laugh and cry with you as my Self, rejoice and mourn with you as my Self. We are in union in the One united mind of God where there is no separation. All that separation seems to show to your awareness has just numbed you to true union and the awareness of who you truly are.

I have been referring to your separated self whom you are holding very close to your heart now and rescuing from its mistaken identity. Yes, this is the you that you seem to be living with daily in the world. This is the you that is being called to wake up and totally be the Christ You. You are already in the Light and you have just temporarily forgotten, so now the memory of your Christ Self is being returned.

It helps so much to love yourself in all its forms, ideas, thoughts and actions. This is what your Christ Self is doing to your mistaken-identity separated self now. It is all one Self, really, but the awareness of this must be reclaimed. In the meantime, as we are doing this together, it is vital to hold your separated self with great love and patience. This is how you are loved by your Creator. Can you comprehend the immense Love that God has for you? Can you receive it? Then, can you, from God, give it to yourself? Love all of you. In no way reject, punish, criticize or judge yourself for forgetting who you are.

Take yourself now in your loving arms and embrace yourself as you would your own child as if it had been totally lost then returned to you. The relief in you both would be so powerful and so deep you would want to hold on to each other for eternity. This is what I am asking you to do from your Christ Self. Hold yourself... your incarnated so-called separate, lost self. You need each other to unite in Knowing. Whenever you feel sad, lonely, doubtful, inadequate or unfulfilled, you are lost. Let your Christ Self find you and hold you so close. I Am that which embraces you in the reunion, the Unity. I am the Christ You, loving and hugging you. The finding of each other when we were separated and lost is the remembering. This is because we are at home together in Union, my beloved. Home is Union. We are reuniting now.

I invite you to read the 23rd Psalm, The Lord is my Shepherd, and bring it into this context now.

Psalm 23   King James Version

"The Lord is my shepherd; I shall not want.
He maketh me to lie down in green pastures.
He leadeth me beside the still waters.
He restoreth my soul.
He leadeth me in the paths of righteousness for His name's sake.
Yea, though I walk through the valley of the shadow of death, I will fear no evil for thou art with me, thy rod and thy staff they comfort me.
Thou preparest a table before me in the presence of mine enemies.
Thou anointest my head with oil, my cup runneth over.
Surely goodness and mercy shall follow me all the days of my life and I will dwell in the house of the Lord for ever."

....

28   AWARENESS

Today, let there be a space in your mind for the peaceful presence of simple awareness. What do we mean by this? Be aware in wholeness with no thoughts. Relax. Relax now as you read this, bringing the simple awareness of simplicity into the moment. Here we are, my beloved, in the simple awareness of Love's Presence together in the awareness of your True Self. This awareness is the way that your being experiences everything in the world and within yourself.

Being aware of awareness is the same as the watcher watching. It is the same state. As you are allowing those old habits of amnesia to fall away and being naturally in your True Self more and more, your awareness of everything is different, is it not? I know you have been thinking a little differently than before and you are aware of yourself from a different place within you. Your commitment to your True Self is guiding you out of your old mistaken and controlling comfort zone into a lighter and non-attached state of mind. You are beginning to know a little of what it feels like to experience from within your presence of Christ.

Can you 'let go' even more? Can you trust even more? I am inviting this of you now. Let us go deeper as if you are walking a step at a time into the sea and are unsure of the next step in case you lose your balance and fall into deep waters. Let us go deeper as if you have entered a dark cave with only a small sliver of light to guide you and you do not know what the next step will bring. The important aspect here is to know you are not alone. You can completely take for granted that I Am with you always and I know each step of the path you are taking. I have said that very statement countless times to all of you in many different writings, songs, poems and prayers. 'I Am with you always'. You can take me for granted. In other words, trust and know I Am with you, and, dear one, you are with your Self. You bring your Self, me, with you wherever you are, whether you are in a body or not. Be aware of this fact, and it is a fact.

When someone leaves their body and so-called 'dies' they leave their body but their eternal essence does not leave them. You are not a body, you are free, you are always with your Self as you were created to be. You take your Self with you. You are always with your Self. I ask you to be more aware of this now. Take this next step into the unknown into the cave of your innermost being. Take the step with your Self, with the me that is the Christ you.

Be aware of your heartbeat, your breath, your thoughts and the Presence of your Self with you always. Walk through your day, step by step in awareness, but without busy thoughts..... just awareness, and in joy. Smile within and let that smile extend as a smile on your face as you pass a brother or sister. Be aware of your smile as a blessing toward them. I am sure when someone has smiled at you in the street and met your eyes you have at times felt blessed, have you not? A little beat skips in your heart and you respond with the same love that has touched you.

Be aware that each encounter with someone is a blessed one. This is a moment of union. Taking the next step into awareness is not as challenging as your fearful ego mind might try to make you think it is. Just step forward and be in awareness. Borrow my awareness if you need it, so you have an example of what I am sharing here. We are in this together. We have never separated. Be aware of this union of Love.

A NOTE FROM ALICE (June 14 2018)

(The day after writing AWARENESS)

I have been asked by Jesus to stop writing for a little while and start reviewing all the chapters so far and take them in deeper, embody and inspirit them. On the subject of Awareness I have been asked to go deeper, to go into the unknown, walk further into the dark cave. I have also been told that I am not alone. How can I truly and completely know this? Do I truly trust in all parts of me that I am not alone? This is what I am going to address now.

I am finding that doubt is coming up again as I am reviewing some of the writings. Doubt makes me feel very low and sad. It depresses me, confines me and tries to wipe out my joy. It makes me feel that receiving these beautiful words from Jesus is delusional, crazy and being made up by some part of me.

I know how I feel when I am writing and re-reading the manuscript. I feel such Oneness, such Unity, such Love. I feel energized, joyful and I start to remember something truly Great within me. I watch myself, just as I have been asked to do but I have conflicts. Who is speaking to me, my ego or my Christ Self? It is at times of doubt like this that putting into practice these wise and beautiful words from Jesus comes into its own.

Is this what you meant me to go through, Jesus, when you asked me to go deeper, into uncomfortable zones of self doubt? Well, I went there, and then I realized that the only thing I can do to help myself is to KNOW I am not alone. I surrender now to someone who is guiding me, loving me and who does know.

I do this and feel at peace. I thank my Self. I am still reviewing and got up at 5:30 am this morning to come to do my review and time with God. Then these beautiful words from Jesus came:

29   GOLDEN THREAD CONNECTION

Neither revelation nor experience can be taught. Revelation is Knowledge joining with you in a Holy Union. Knowledge is of God and is part of what you have forgotten but have never lost. You DO know yourSelf. You Do know God. As you remember this, Knowledge is revealed to you once again and it comes from the direct Inner Experience of Union.

I cannot give you direct experience in these words, but I can extend an invitation for you to open yourself to be willing to Know. Are you willing, truly willing? This is not intellectual, not of the intellect, but of the Heart, the very Heart of your Eternal Spirit. As you know your Eternal Spirit, you know your Self. Be aware of your Eternal Spirit always with you like a living golden thread connected to your Source. The eternal connection has never been broken and never will be. Let this golden thread become an experience for you, a direct experience. I invite you to be with this in silence for a while.

In the silent communion your connection is revealed to you.

Melt into it. Surrender totally to the experience. Allow yourself a new way of perceiving everything. Allow yourself to trust the Source of your Golden Thread. Allow the Golden Thread to be the Source of your awareness where you are fed with everything that is Truth. Reconnect, my beloved, to your awareness of connection.

As your Whole True Self connects, revelation brings the complete Knowledge of who you are, your origins and the Harmony of the Love that you are. Connection is such a harmonious homecoming. Each time you choose to connect, you remember. It is actually very simple and very real. Revelation is your Spirit waking you up. It is direct connection experiencing you and giving you your Self.

All illusions and problems of the world fall away from you as you connect. When you re-enter the world of your body, its needs and the demands of the world, you have brought this connection into your life and through this all else is affected. This is the realm of miracle, the change not only of your mind but of the whole of you, back to your Self.

Does this reveal something of the Knowledge that I am sharing and giving you? You are forever connected to your Holy Source. The Source of Love is feeding you beyond your understanding. This is the way you are meant to be in your unfoldment, in your world. This Golden Thread is your Source and life-line and has never left you. I invite you to use it and then revelation is yours.

....

You and I in our Christ Self are co-creating a new world, a new reality now. You are undoing your mistaken identity, ideas and beliefs about yourself and you are becoming who you truly are, who your Creator always meant you to be. In your time line you are unwinding a past that seemed separated, a past that was created from a separated idea of an upside down world. We are now co-creating together by undoing illusion and, with Love, remembering Eternal Truth.

Within your committed choice to know who you truly are, you have called forth the Power within you and the Powers around you to fulfill your vision of knowing your True Self. There is more, as you know and feel, yet you are already reaping the harvest of the seeds of Love and commitment that you planted by calling forth this Joining. This is co-creating.

How delightful these times together are. How easy, peaceful and light are our unions in dialogue, communion and writing. It is all written in the stars already, you know. Yes it is. The stars know your destiny and they help lay the foundations of the path you travel, as we have referred before to them lighting the path. Like other Presences, the stars within you and outside of you are your guides and friends. Talk to the stars, the beings that live there do hear your star-heart communications and they love you.

As we have shared, you have such power, such gifts, such creative energy that your Creator thought into you. It is hard to comprehend it all and it is enough just to know it is there. In co-creation the memories are stirred and your Power is used. You are made by Love to create more Love. You are made by your Creator to create....... to co-create together and spread Heavenly awareness all through your Spirit.

You do not stop at the awareness of who you are, you extend it through co-creating in the Grace of Love's Embrace. This is so, even if you cannot fully understand or absorb it all. It is so. This is Love in action, God's world in Joy, your Heart extended and embraced in the One. As your Spirit laughs in Home coming, I laugh with you as we co-create together in our union.

....

31   RELAX IN LOVE

Relax in Love, it is a very safe place to be. When you are in Love you are totally safe and can truly relax, relax and let go into your Self. When you are relaxed and stress-free there is no fear. Instead there is a peaceful Joy. This is the state of Heaven and in this state we merge in Oneness. It is also time to remember the Living Golden Thread of your connection which energizes and empowers your state of remembering. It is this remembering we are 'working' with here, remembering your True Christ Self in a state of relaxed Love.

I ask you to surrender to your deep Knowing where you know that you know. Allow and trust that state to take you over now. Call forth your Knowing from deep within you. You would not even be reading or writing this now if you did not Know. So, know that you Know. Now, allow Love in this Peaceful place to totally embrace you as you float in it. Everything you 'see', 'touch', and 'feel' is of Light, which is the 'form' of Heaven's Realm. Your Knowing knows Light and its living Presence. Your Knowing knows the safety of Heaven. Your Knowing knows the relaxation that Love brings. This is also the peaceful mind, the still mind of God, your Creator who created you in the 'image' of Love's Light.

Light is not of your world of form as you know it, yet everything is of Light. There is no darkness or shadow in God's world because there is no duality. Duality is the first cause of separation. Heaven, your true Home, is non-dual. It is in non-duality you can truly relax because nothing is pulling you in any direction.

To relax in Love is to relax in non-duality. It is here that healing can truly take place. It is here, in Light that you are as you have always been, as you were created. Your Eternal Spirit is aware of your Earthly life totally and is inviting you to bring relaxation in Love into it as often as you can remember to do so. Feed yourself with it. The living Golden Thread is such a part of this for it nourishes your relaxation from the Loving Source.

You need constant reminders of this state, just like you need to eat food, drink water, sleep, rest and look after yourself. To relax in Love is your true state. It is important to tune into your true state as often as you are able to because it is by doing so that you are connected to your True Self.

There are many ways to keep remembering and I will use as many as it takes to get you there. Step by step, breath by breath, memory by memory, we are doing this together. We are holding your child-like 'separated self' so close that you are at One in your Heart as you relax in Love and are in Peace now.

....

32)   BE STILL AND KNOW

Be still and know that you are God. You are a hologram of the Divine. When you are still, within, you give your Self a space to be. In the hustle and bustle of your busy world, to be truly still is more important than it has ever been for your peace of mind. It is vital to pause from what you think you know and what you think you are and be still and know you are as God created you.

This knowing takes no effort. All it takes is a simple choice. The famous Shakespeare quote " To be or not to be, that is the question" could be more plainly expressed, " To be who I truly am or not to be who I truly am, that is the question." That is the choice. Feel this. It is, actually, very simple.

In your dual awareness there are only really two choices. You have heard this before: the choice of love or fear. You either choose to be in fear, in your ego/liar self in separation, or to be in Love in your Christ Self in Oneness. Do you see? Can you feel the extreme split within you between the two states of mind? Each state, fear or love, is a state of mind as it is all within you. In one state you have forgotten who you are, therefore you are lost and not expressing your True Self. In the other state you remember who you are, therefore you are expressing your God or Christ Self as you were originally created.

The choice, the commitment to be your genuine Christ Self should be easy for you, so why does it seem so difficult? It seems difficult because the liar has so programmed your mind to be diverted from your Self that you have simply forgotten. Have you ever, with all positive intention, started something you know is going to help you in some way, and then got completely diverted from it? The diversion is subtle, it is insidious. The ego/liar is insidious, it is subtly influencing you away from your positive intention. This happens over and over again until you recognize it. You recognize the diversion by being the observer, the watcher, as I have mentioned many times. When you recognize that you have been diverted, it is not so subtle, instead it is visible to your awareness and you realize you have a choice. Not only do you have a choice, you have help from a Presence that you forgot was always there to be with you and for you.

All it takes is an instant, a miracle instant or what you would call an "Ah Ha" moment. This miracle moment is a step outside your time and space and becomes a revelation, a moment of Grace. That moment, because it is outside your time and space, is of God and it is real and it is used in your waking up, your remembering. In that moment, that Holy Instant of remembering, all insidious intentions of the liar, of fear and separation, are dissolved instantly. You are aware of your Self surrounded by and being within the Divine Presence.

Divine Presence is all there is. Everything else that seems to be diverting you from knowing this falls away as the illusion that it is, the nothing that it is. The ego/liar has based everything you have thought was something on nothing. Its bubble has burst and you are left with your Original God Self within Divine Presence.

Be still and know. Be still and remember. Be still and receive from yourself the Presence of your Self. Even as you read these simple words now, the Presence resurrects within your awareness and you know. Be still, my beloved, and be in that Knowing. I AM with you. God is with you. You are totally with your Self. Be still, be still and be completely with your Self.

....

33 HOME

Home.... what do I mean when I use the word Home and refer to it constantly? Home is your origins, your original created state of being that you think you left but never really did and never really could. You think you left when you 'split from God'. It was only a thought, a mad idea that you created that produced duality and that split you. The True You, your True Eternal Self can never be split, but an idea split off from the Eternal You and this 'idea' is what you are now experiencing in your seeming everyday world. This so-called split or separated self (which, by the way, you are holding and hugging very close to your heart now in complete love) has been witnessing itself 'living' what is not its Home in a time line created by the separation that does not exist at 'Home.'

In the mad idea of separation everything was turned inside out and upside down. The split produced duality. It also created the body. Whenever anything is split or separated from its original state it becomes something else. Look at what happened when the atom was split! The evidence of the consequences of separation and splitting is everywhere in the liar/ego's world that you exist in. Separation is not of God. Unity is of God. Unity is your Home.

When you leave home you go out into the world and experience yourself in various worldly situations. You feel you must survive, earn your way, pay for things, prove yourself and countless other perceptions you have when 'leaving' Home. You learn what it is like to live in a crazy world and you forget your Self. You are pulled in many split directions to live in the separated world away from Home. You have a great need to 'prove' yourself to yourself and to others. Somewhere, though, you know something is wrong. Something is wrong with what you see, how the separated world is set up, how you have to earn your right to exist and so on. Fear becomes your conscious and unconscious companion because of your seeming need to 'survive.' Sometimes you are 'high' in your life and sometimes you are' low'. You can have busy, busy thoughts and voices in your mind, telling you that you are one thing or another. You become confused and stressed. Intermingled with all this you have relationships in many forms. Relationships with things, people and places. First you relate to yourself (or not), then friends, work mates, family members and lovers. Each relationship you have reflects a different aspect of yourself to you, a part of yourself you have not accepted or integrated or been conscious of, so you project dislike and eventually aggression toward someone you think is outside and separate from yourself. You become the victim of your own projections and then blame what you have projected and separated from. It gets more and more split as you see others separate from you and so dismiss them. Or you see someone you want to love and you unite with them and include them.

On and on it goes, until you start waking up and remembering Home where none of these seemingly unsafe experiences took place, where peace was where discord is now. Where Love was where conflict is now and where Union was where projected separation is now. The state of Home calls you to remember your Holy Self before the mad idea of separation. What a relief! However, in the meantime, what the separation seems to have done or created must be undone or uncreated. This undoing is called The Atonement. The at-one-meant. It is meant that you return to the One.

When your mad idea separated you and created your body, your Creator gave you the most loving of gifts. You were given the Voice for God, the Holy Spirit, to bridge the void between Home and the separation. The bridge, the Holy Spirit, was always and is still now available as the Voice of Truth, the Voice of Love, Grace and Sanity. By listening to and uniting with the Holy Spirit you have started to remember your Home, your original Self as you were created.

I united fully with the Voice for God and remembered my Christ Self and because I did that the Holy Spirit and I have the same identity. The Voice for God, who can never leave you, is the Christ or the Holy Spirit within you that Knows who it truly is and is your Home. Your Christ Self is your Voice for God, your bridge and healer, your identity and in your Christ Self you are at Home.

So here we are, my beloved Christ Self, together in Knowledge and united in Love, remembering our Home, our origins and our original state of Oneness, of Unity. We are undoing and in that undoing remembering more and more the Christ Self we are in God's Holy Home.

....

34.   THE CONCEPT OF LACK

When you had the mad idea to separate from Home or Heaven, duality was created. Lack was also created. The feeling of lack is a strong fear in everyone in the separated world. Lack IS separation because you have been split off from your Self and you feel a lack of your Self. In the Oneness of your Self there is no lack, no idea of lack whatsoever. Lack does not exist because you are in the Knowledge of Wholeness where there is peace within you. When you have inner peace, you lack nothing.

It is possible on Earth to have this feeling, this awareness. As you unite in your awareness with your true Self, your Christ Self, you are more at peace about everything. You can be at peace knowing the dramas of the world are but puffs of smoke, clouds that temporarily block the Light.

Lack comes in many forms. You are well familiar with the financial one and there is also the lack of time, of confidence, of food, of security and of understanding. There is the lack of loving yourself and others, the lack of peace, of joy, of awareness and so on. Unconsciously lack rules most people. This is because they have split with their Creator, their Great Provider, and they feel the lack of Unity.

As you are remembering your Self more and more, you also remember you are totally cared for. In the state of Heaven there is nothing to want, nothing to lack so even the fear or thought of lack is non-existent. What could your Christ Self possibly lack? Being in your Christ Self you are in total Peace. Peace comes with your Knowledge of your Self. Being in total Peace there are no needs or wants. Each moment of now is full and each now is taken care of. There is no time, so therefore there is no such concept as 'not enough' or 'lack of time'. Can you imagine being in a state where time is not in any way an issue? Well, it is not and never has been an issue when you are Home in your Christ Identity.

These are not just lofty ideas or dreams, my beloved. They are, as always, reminders, so that you can bring them into your thoughts and they can help you undo your mistaken beliefs. This moment, as you are reading these words, you are in complete wholeness in the timeless awareness of abundance, contentment and Peace. There is no lack, no need whatsoever to want or need anything.

Know, as you go about your everyday tasks that are running through your life that there is total security in the Peace of God. I know that this may not seem easy because it may appear that in your ego world you need this or that. Those are temporary needs and they are ultimately looked after. Ask for any fear for the future to be replaced by grateful knowing that you are covered, you are provided for. Where you are at One with the Will of God there is a way (where there is a will there is a way). Unite with who you are, Christ, and you are automatically united with the Loving and Abundant Will of God. Be still now and know this, my beloved, and in the knowing remember your Christ Self is at Peace in Wholeness, Abundance and Gratitude. All is well. Let it Be.

It is interesting, is it not, how easy it is to be diverted and distracted away from the awareness of your Self? The (ego) world is a strong magnet that pulls you away from remembering. There is, of course, within you, at your core, the seed or essence of your true Christ Self. That seed can never leave and is with you always whether you are in the world in a body or not in a body. This seed is like a huge, bright star condensed into your very soul where your spirit dwells. Even now, as you become aware of this star seed a part of you responds with joy and wants to commune with it.

Let us do that now. Be still and know you are always as you were originally created. Now, imagine your creation and God extending to create an expression of Love called Christ You. The Great Seed of perfect Light was planted and you became the bright Light of Christ..... the extension of your Creator. Feel your Star Seed. Know it. As you relate to your Christ Star Seed Self you open and expand as if you are a beautiful flower that has just been watered. You expand and make your Light known to your Self. You remember your creation, your becoming. The Star Seed Christ You knows exactly who you are and is ready to shine your Light towards Your Self. In doing so you acquire a Sight that allows your vision to know your Self as one with all of Divine creation, all of Light, all of Love.

Your Star Seed has now been 'watered' by you, by your remembering. It is always a part of you. Now, as you read these words, remember your Golden Thread to Source. Visualize it connected within your bright Star Seed. As you expand in this knowing you are feeding your spirit. You are not being diverted or pulled by the strong magnet of the ego world, you are transported directly to your Christ Light.

I ask you now to be at peace and feed this awareness by being in it in the stillness for a while. As you do this the resting Light within you awakes and radiates throughout all of your body, mind and spirit. Go forth now in your daily life in the awareness of the Flower of your Star shining all through you. Through your Christ Star eyes you will have inner and outer sight and love will be all your vision.

....

36   GRATITUDE

To be grateful is a blessed state indeed. Gratitude brings forth joy and peace with your heart. It calls forth a Divine receptivity in your spirit that enables you to feel the power and the presence of Grace.

When you are at peace, a natural feeling of gratitude embraces you in a way that helps the awareness of deep and Divine abundance to surround you. Your Christ Self is always in gratitude, always in the Grace of peace of mind because it knows it is at Home in God.

I am sure there have been times when you have felt discontent, depressed and complaining about everything. These are traits of the ego/liar who can never be satisfied or content. Its motto is 'Seek but do not ever find'. The miracle-minded moment can come in an instant of a change of mind from this sadness and discontent to the peaceful joy of gratitude. Gratitude automatically brings with it a love for yourself because it is part of the Golden Thread to Source.

When you are witnessing, for example, a very beautiful sunset and you are in momentary awe of the vast beauty of the colours, the stillness and movement of light in the sunset, you are in an open state of receptivity. In this state gratitude surrounds you like a loving embrace from your deepest spirit. This is a moment of Grace. It is also Love extending itself from you and towards you. Gratitude is an extension of the Christ Self that you are. It is a true exchange where giving and receiving meet and in the meeting moment you know you are blessed.

Grace and Gratitude are like partners in the awareness of your Christ Self, my beloved. As we, in this moment, are giving and receiving from each other, we are full of the Presence of the Grace of Gratitude. This is allowing your connection to your Source to fill you up, and just be with it. This is the state of communion. Communion, Grace and Gratitude feed you on all levels and then you can feed others as you have allowed yourself to be fed. This is the way of harmony and brings you such joy that your cup runneth over.

If, at any time, you are influenced by a discontented state, it is worth your whole peace of mind to ask for gratitude instead of this. I WANT THE PEACE OF GOD ---- and within that Peace you have the great bonus of gratitude. In turn, gratitude gives you all you are and brings Christ Sight automatically.

In this moment I am deeply grateful to you, my beloved Christ Self, for taking time out of your worldly mind and bringing it into the awareness of your Heavenly one. Here we meet and here we are at peace. Here we know our Self together in the Love and abundance of Divine Grace. Gratitude has opened you to this Grace.

....

37   RELATIONSHIP

Everything is meant to be in relationship with everything else. This inter-relationship in the highest sense is what brings the awareness of Oneness. Relationship and Oneness are like a partnership in the great scheme of things because ultimately it is through relationship that Oneness will be a true realization for you. Without relationship everything both in spirit and in matter would fall apart because separation would make it do so. Relationship fits, and is like a puzzle where everything can fit together and become one great whole.

Let us start with the core relationship, the inter-relationship between you and God, you and your Creator. From this primary relationship everything is sourced. " Seek ye first the Kingdom of Heaven and all things will be given unto you." Your relationship with God is your heavenly state where everything else comes from. Everything. This, your Christ Self knows as Its Source. All other relationships that you have, stem from this primary one and are meant to be like holograms of your inter-relationship with your Source. Your birthright of Divine Abundance comes about through relationship. Nothing can exist without relating to everything around it. That is why separation cannot exist in reality.

In the world there are the seeds of the possibility of Heaven. This potential of Heaven on Earth is based on how true relationship, in Divine Harmony, is meant to be. Everything in its state of expression, be it a tree, an animal, a stone, the air, wind, the food you eat, the sights you see, the words you use to communicate with, each expression of life is in communication with each other. It is the only way that life, in the greater sense of what life truly is, can exist.

In separation the liar/ego has made distorted relationships and instead of co-operation and harmony, chaos has happened. Inter-relationship can never stop happening, it is impossible. However, from the upside-down, separated ego perspective, true relationship has been forgotten for what it is and what you witness as an insane, disharmonious and chaotic world is the result. This separation is caused by the need to control because of fear. Fear only exists in separation. It cannot exist in union for that is impossible. True relationship has been forgotten for what it is and in its place there has been competition and expressions of duality (for example ´me and them´ instead of 'us'). Separation has been trying and is still trying to break down inter-relationship. It is this attempt to break down the natural relationship within the One that causes such insanity, chaos and destruction in the temporal ego world.

Now, my beloved, we are in relationship with each other in the awareness of our Christ Identity. In this awareness the original relationship is remembered between you and your Source. There is only Harmony, Love, Simplicity and Peace in true relationship but there is also the knowing and loving of your True Self in its original natural state where it knows nothing else but Its Self. In your knowing of your true Christ Self you have no other identity. You automatically relate to everyone from this Source and they to you. From the Source you are in Oneness. Individual personal relationships are meant to echo the original relationship you have with your Source. This is the natural way. It is the way of Heaven.

Only in distorted relationship does the world stop working as a harmonious whole. Only when Oneness is forgotten are your relationships with your brothers and sisters threatened and at war. There is no reason, and I repeat NO reason, no matter how the ego/ liar wants to justify it, for anything to be out of harmonious inter- relationship. Think for a moment, how, even in the smallest ways, you justify your separation by judging and controlling a situation or person. You do this by wanting it or them to be other than what they are. How insane is that? Either you can relate to everything from fear, which is the separation, or from love which is the union in Oneness. Both use relationship, one as God created you and one as you try unsuccessfully to create from your separated self.

So, any kind of existence or life depends upon relationship. Your Creator created you to be in relationship the way your Source is in relationship with you. There is no greater relationship than this. It is the foundation for all relationships. It is worth your while to spend your quiet moments in the inner awareness of the relationship you have with God. All things then come from that perfect harmony. You and I within our relationship are an extension of this, my beloved. So it is and always will be... Love extending ItSelf through and with all creation.

....

38   FORGIVENESS

To forgive is to go forward positively and cleanly. Forgiveness is the great cleaning, the great healing principle towards your own awareness of your True Self. Your Christ Self forgives in every moment like a refreshing breath. Forgiveness is the pure breath of your heart loving you. To love yourself is to forgive and to forgive is to love your Self.

The old way of holding on, being resentful, unforgiving and attached to the past never works for anyone. So why choose to be in this state of mind? Why dislike yourself so much as to not let go of the past? The past is gone, so it is non-existent. To the ego/liar mind this is not true, but then the ego mind is a liar and everything it thinks is counter-productive. Forgiveness always involves a past situation, even if it was only moments ago. When you can accept the past as gone and therefore non-existent, forgiveness is as natural as every breath in the now. When you forgive you heal yourself and therefore know your Self.

When I gave you what you call the Lord's Prayer I invited you to receive the unconditional forgiveness and love of God so that you can equally give forgiveness in the same way you received it from God. When you forgive another for mis-takes (or debts/trespasses) your mis-takes are automatically forgiven too. Forgiveness is for your own healing, your own awakening. In the light of forgiveness the light shines on your Christ Self. It is a natural stepping stone to being in the state of Heaven where forgiveness is not necessary because everything is already clean and cleared. The incredible peace that forgiveness gives cannot be emphasized enough. Forgiveness opens the doorway to inner peace of mind.

You must first accept that the past is over, gone, and therefore now non-existent. You can always ask for help to realize this. All your past is gone, like a breath is gone right after you have breathed it. Would you or even could you go backwards and re-live a past breath? Of course not! Breathing is now and gone, now and gone, now and gone and it keeps you present to who you are. This is why I shared that when you have an awareness of your breath, your breath can become one of your best friends.

It is impossible to go backwards and bring back a breath you let go of a while ago. It is equally impossible to hang on to any past experience and expect it to be real. It is gone. When you know that, forgiveness is easy and flows naturally. Use your breath as you forgive and be free. You are not meant to be in your own created hell of past pain. It is insane. What I am doing here is inviting you to the state of Heaven and therefore clearing everything in its way.

If you have any past pain or resentment, invite your Heavenly Christ Self to breath through you and help you forgive and be at peace. Just ask. Be willing to ask and be willing to be instantly free and at peace. Are you willing? Of course you are! How could you not be?

Let forgiveness, therefore, be as easy as breathing for you. It is your gift to yourself in every moment of now.

You are Love. You are Free.

You are Forgiven. You are at Peace.

You are Christ in Heaven.

....

39   BE AT PEACE

Be at Peace ----- the Peace that goes beyond understanding and the Peace that gives you the Knowledge that you are One with the Christ that you are. Peace be with you. It is your true nature. As Peace surrounds you inwardly and outwardly you know automatically (even without thinking you know) you are as God created you, Christ, in union, in Peace with your Creator.

All problems, stresses and blockages melt away in the presence of true Peace, and you are free. This is your natural state and any other state is an impostor. Your mind is meant to be at peace, to relate from peace and to give and receive peace. Instead, you have allowed the liar impostor to temporarily inhabit your mind and fill it with everything that creates forgetfulness to the Presence of Peace.

When you know this and accept it as fact, you can start watching the impostors, for they are visible to your awareness. As you watch whatever disturbs your peace you can think again and choose peace instead of the usurper.

Try to watch your mind and those thoughts that divert your peace. It takes time to get used to this because of your habit of fearful and defensive thoughts. The ego/liar needs to defend itself constantly in very clever and disguised ways. It thinks it has to be separate and protect itself from anything that is not of its limited belief system. Everything that it believes needs constant defence because it is a lie. The lying mind has become such a habit, such a blind habit, that it has forgotten it can be at peace.

'I want Peace instead of this' is a prayer and a statement of remembering. In this, peace is offered and you know you can choose it--- or not. Why wouldn't you? Why wouldn't you want peace instead of fear, defence and attack? Why do you attack? You attack because you feel threatened and because you have forgotten who you are. In forgetting who you are, you defend the lie and then you attack.

I was attacked and crucified by forgetfulness. No one would attack or harm another while remembering a peaceful mind. You are the Child of God, Christ. Who, in their right Mind would attack their fellow Christ Self ? The Peace that comes from this dissolves all need to attack and defend.

In Peace, all that is not of Peace is non-existent and never was. The illusion of fear is no more. Be at Peace, my beloved, and remember who you are. Step back from all that is not of Peace and let your Christ Self lead the way.

....

40   LOVING YOUR SEPARATED SELF AWAKE

Together, as who we are, Christ, we hold and love your forgetfulness. We hold and love and forgive your separated mind thoughts. We hold and love and forgive the insane world in its mistaken perception. We hold and love as God is eternally and lovingly holding everything in perfect Oneness.

In these sacred moments of communion, aware of the Golden Thread to our loving Creator, I ask you to remember to hold yourself close to your heart. I ask you to hold all of yourself with your Christ Power, your Christ Connection, your Christ Love, your Christ Inclusiveness and your Christ Healing. You are Christ hugging yourself back to the awareness of your Self. In this embrace of Self you are waking up to the state of Heavenly Awareness. Heavenly Awareness is the living experience of your true senses. In your body you have five senses. Heavenly senses are vast and sight is more than seeing with your physical eyes. Sight is seeing and knowing with your Christ eyes. What does this mean? As you see with your Christ eyes you are aware of That which created you as an extension of ItSelf. As your Christ Self, know you are as God created you. Your sight, your awareness is an extension of God. You are Christ----

the Child of God. All those you encounter are also the Child of God. They are all your brothers and sisters in God.

As Jesus I realized this and became Jesus Christ. I was already Christ, as you are, but I needed to awaken to my True Self. Now I accompany you in the same, equal realization. I invite you to use your real eyes, your Christ eyes, your Christ sight.

In your Christ Self you hold, as a mother holds her beloved baby, the experience of your separated self. You are uniting with who you are as you are coming Home to the awareness of it. *IN THE MEANTIME, UNTIL YOU STEP FULLY INTO THE AWARENESS OF WHO YOU TRULY ARE, IT IS VITAL THAT YOUR SEPARATED SELF KNOWS IT IS CONSTANTLY HELD, INCLUDED AND ETERNALLY, UNCONDITIONALLY LOVED BY YOUR TRUE SELF.*

Be in the Light of Awareness of your Christ Self now. Breathe in this perfect truth. You are your own saviour. Your remembering is your awakening. You do remember, so you can stop pretending from your liar mind that you don't. In your state of awakened light, embrace the you who temporarily sleeps in forgetfulness. Love her totally. Hold her close to your Christ Heart. Sing the Song of Eternal Love as an awakening song to the ear of your worldly self. Do you hear it? Do you hear yourself singing? It is the Voice of God singing in harmony now as you receive the embrace of Christ Love.

You are your own Mother holding the child of yourself, teaching it who it truly is. You are your own Mother/Christ holding, nourishing the choice of awakening within you. The song is familiar, it is the song of Home, of Heaven. Let it guide you on the starry pathway of joy, my beloved. I am singing with you and loving witnessing your Christ Self hugging you awake.

....

41   SURRENDER AND RECEIVE YOURSELF

The question " Who am I?" has been asked inside the mind of humans since they could think. Now you know who you are, Christ, the original extension of God as you were created to be in pure communion. Now what? Now that in words you have been told who you are, what do you do with this Knowledge? How do you live, be and express your Christ Self?

The first experience is to be still, very still in mind and body and receive, just receive. Receive your Self from Who created you. To receive your Self is to surrender, totally and completely. Surrender as if your very life depended upon it. Your True Life, your True Self does depend upon it. Surrendering is not a giving up, it is a giving over. Giving over to a greater Knowing. That means you surrender everything you think you know and completely clear your slate of how you have defined yourself. You let go of any beliefs or ideas of who you think you are. You do not know from the mind or thought system you have been used to listening to.

The ego/liar hates the idea of surrendering because it has nothing to hang on to. All its false beliefs have dissolved instantly in your surrender. It is helpless. When the ego/liar is helpless you realize immediately the illusion and the lies it has based itself on. Surrender, complete surrender is the quickest path to waking up. It is also the state of clear receptivity.

I know this from experience and I am passing on my experience here to you. Actually, even the concept of experience itself is let go of. There are no words to explain total surrender. You have surrendered all words, definitions, ideas, expectations, thoughts and concepts. In fact everything you have been used to as building blocks of what you have created yourself to be must be surrendered.

This surrendering has been feared and avoided by you for a long, long time. It has seemed a threat because the ego is so afraid of being exposed for what it is. It is nothing pretending to be everything. In total surrender the ego, then, dissolves into the nothing that it is. So who is surrendering? Who is giving over? Your original Self. Your pure non-dual Self in Oneness with your Source. That is who is surrendering. You are surrendering to and with your True Self.

In this total state of surrender you can now clearly receive your Self. Time dissolves. It does not exist, like so many other things you have been used to. Everything that is not permanent is not real. The question, " Who am I?" is being answered by eliminating everything you are not. So, what is left? What is left after everything that is not permanent is gone and all concepts of what you thought you are have dissolved? Your Original Self as God created you. Receive Your Self as God has given you. Receive the Self you have always been and always will be. The Self you now know as your Christ Self is like a new relationship you get to know again. You need not 'fall' in love with your Self, instead rise in Love with the Greatness of your Being. You are made by and from Love, so love what you are made from. When you know you are made by Love ItSelf you can express your Self as that Love, that God Love.

I will help you surrender. I will, in fact, surrender with you and we end up in our original creation together as we always have been. Receive your Self now. It has always been and always will be Love extending ItSelf as You.

....

42   ABANDON

Will you abandon yourself to your Self? Will you so relax and trust that you let go as if you are going over at your 'dying' moment? Let go, you are in my loving arms, the 'arms' of love, safety and acceptance. I fully accept you with or without any ideas you have of yourself. You are accepted totally by me because I know you as you were originally created. I know you as Myself. I know MySelf when I abandon totally to Love who knows me as ItSelf. We are in this together and always have been. Within your individuation you are choosing to be in the One that you are.

Truth is abstract. It is a paradox of abstract Knowledge greater and simpler than anything you can grasp or understand. In the greatness of Truth you can only abandon yourself. Surrender and abandon yourself. This is a key to open you to who you are.

"How can I abandon so totally yet live in a body in the world?", I hear your mind ask. You abandon inwardly and watch yourself. You live in the world outwardly and watch yourself. You watch yourself from the 'eyes' of what you have abandoned to. You watch yourself from what you have surrendered to. That is the 'sight' of your Christ Self. Try this now.

Be aware of your body reading this now. Look at it. It has been fed. It has been moving, speaking, living in the world as it is. At the moment it is still and quiet as it is reading this with its physical eyes. Now, be aware of your mind, your thoughts, these words as you read them. You are experiencing and aware of your body and your mind. You are also within the Presence. Feel it gently yet ever so powerfully with you. It never leaves you, you just seem to leave it in your awareness. The Presence is your Christ Self and it has Eternal Sight whenever you choose to use it. This is your Observer, your loving witness, your watcher. It is your true Self witnessing all of you with no attachment, judgement or demands. This Presence of your Self you are experiencing is also what you have just trusted and abandoned to, even though it seems for a short time. It is safe and easy and all it takes is a present moment of abandoned trust. You now know how to live in the world in a body while watching your mind and letting go into your Eternal Self.

You will always come Home to Your Self, my beloved, because there is no other Self. You need not die in your body to do this because you are doing it now. What I am sharing with you is how to be in this awareness while still in an earthly body, using your thoughts that come from your earthly experience and yet still being aware of your Eternal Self. Abandon, let go. It is safe, easy and is what you truly desire. So give your Self your Self, in your abandonment to the Presence of your Christ Love.

....

43 IMAGINATION AND INTUITION

Imagination and intuition are like two friends travelling together on a journey to the same destination. Imagination is the vastness of your awareness speaking with you in the universal language of images, images that come to life within you as you receive them from your intuition. Your intuition is God speaking within you. Of course God speaks with you. You are an extension of God. You are and always have been linked, so God is communicating with you as your True Self, as your God Self, your Christ Self. Your intuition is your inner voice. It has been called by many names, the Higher Self, the Holy Spirit, your Guide, the still small voice and many others. It does not matter what it is called. It is present as The Presence and is always a part of who you are.

Your intuition loves to play with you through your imagination and your imagination is your birthright, your creative tool to experience your Self. God used Divine imagination in creating you, and it is one of your ultimate tools in co -creating with your Creator.

As you read this, do you not find it exciting to have the freedom to co-create with your Creator, using your imagination? Where do you think the language of images comes from originally? Your Creator is constantly extending through the all-inclusive language of imagination. Imagination has no boundaries and no separation. It is in a constant state of timeless extension.

The ego/liar has misused imagination for its own purposes and has planted false images, false concepts and separate lying ideas within you. It has tried to block your intuition and Divine imagination by pretending to be something it is not. This is part of your forgetfulness. The liar has even downgraded imagination and sought to eliminate it by trying to destroy your use of it. The liar knows the power of Divine imagination and has tried to separate you from it. This is why you often hear, "Well, it is only your imagination". The ego/liar has wanted to separate you from everything you truly are and put you in a state of amnesia where you forget your intuition and your imagination. What hell that would be! What hell that truly is in the upside down world of the ego.

When you are the witness or watcher you can plainly see the lie, the false ideas planted by the separated self to stop you remembering who you are. Your intuition is communicating with you through the Golden Thread lifeline. Give it free access inside you to express itself. Listen to your intuition in everything. Your intuition unites with its good friend imagination and together they help you express your Divine Identity, your True Self. This is such good news for the self that has forgotten itSelf. Intuition and imagination remind you of your vastness, your never-ending creativity, co-creating with your Creator.

I know this is so and I use imagination with you as you are writing and reading these words now. Words can be like a paint brush writing in the language of images. I love your receptivity to this because through your receiving from me you are receiving your Self. I use the language of imagination all the time because I know it is an extension of my Self as God created me. I am also one with my intuition because I know that the Voice of God is True.

I am using imagination and intuition as we write together and am joyous that you are open to our Eternal Union. How would you like to use your imagination to co-create with God and me right now? It is like being given a wish you know will come true, is it not? Imagine, then, a wish that your Christ Self has. What would you like that to be? I hear your wish, it becomes a prayer, a voice to God from you. Your wish is that all souls know and remember their Self as who they are, their Christ Self as God created them.

Your wish, your prayer, your vision through your language of images is not only heard, it is unfolding, my beloved. Keep your communication lines open through intuition and imagination. Grace and Miracles are your inheritance. So be it.

....

I have referred to Heaven a great deal and will continue doing so. Heaven is a word that symbolizes not a 'place' but a state of being in God's Holy Home. It is your Home in God. It is your original and eternal state of being where you, I and all of us dwell in perfect Oneness.

There are no words to explain Heaven for it is beyond words but I will remind you of it often. You are meant to live in Heaven on Earth in the awareness of your Divine Holiness. Heaven has no walls, no doors, no boundaries and no time. It is Love constantly extending ItSelf In Divine Creative Expression. It is where you are created to dwell in the state of Love. It is your Home state. It is where your true Self dwells in eternity and it is where you have always known who you truly are.

All it takes, my beloved, to be in the state of Heaven is to remember your Self. Being in the remembrance of your Self IS being Home. You often have peaceful moments when a rush of great Love comes over you and Heaven is your experience. The Harmony, Love, Peace and Joy in this state are all your eternal birthright. Your Christ Self knows this and lives constantly in the state of Heaven. Use your Christ awareness now to remember Heaven. I invite you to be still and invite your Christ Self to be in the Peace of Heaven. Your Christ Self knows this well as it dwells constantly in the state of Heaven. Be there now with the Christ You and bring it into your everyday life.

You can bring Heaven into everything you think, do, feel and are. I keep repeating, it is your natural state. My beloved, receive Heaven's Presence into you more than you have ever done. Open to Its generosity of Harmony and Bliss. It is yours and always has been. It is the state of constant Grace. You do not need in any way to earn Heaven, all you need to do is to choose it. No man, church or organization has any authority or right to tell you for any reason that you cannot 'go to Heaven'. It is your Home and your origin and no man-made rules or doctrines can state that you deserve to go to Heaven (or hell).

As I have said, Heaven is a state of being, a state of mind, a state of awareness. All it takes to know your Home is to change your mind about how you are and who you are. How you are is as God created you. Who you are is Christ. From these statements, these truths, you are on the timeless express space vehicle to your Heavenly Home.

Here we are together. You are One in your Christ Self in Heaven. Now remember and bring that awareness into your life. In Love's Sight, Heaven is everywhere.

....

45   THE STARRY PATH OF LIGHT

Sometimes I have referred to the Starry Path. This is an image of the Way of Light and of Truth that will always lead you out of darkness. When I use the word darkness I refer to the areas in your mind and thoughts that have been temporarily taken over by the ego and have caused you to forget who you are. You can instantly and joyously relate to the image of the Starry Path, a path made of stars, because it is a delightful image of Light. The Starry Path reveals itself to you when you feel lost and need help to find your way back home after being confused and helpless.

The Starry Path, or the Guidance of Light, is linked to your Golden Thread Connection because they are both ways to remember your Divine Connection. As you wake up, or remember, you get straight back into direct connection with your Source. You know the story of the Prodigal Son, it is an important parable I shared to show you where you have been in separation and how your Creator, at Home in Heaven, celebrates your return. God is complete unconditional Love and is your Home, your origins. You thought you separated from Heaven when you had the mad idea to leave. It was only an idea that you believed. Now you have caught yourself and are holding that self close. You are choosing the path of Light to guide you. I invite you to re-read 'Love's Portal' once again so you remember you are holding yourself.

Often you have heard of those who have experienced death of the body and have received such love, such guidance that they feel the need to share the experience of Truth as much as they can. I tell you now that you do not need to have a near-death experience or even to leave your body completely to know this Love. I show you the Starry Path, the way of Light to lead you from the darkness of forgetfulness to remembering your Self.

Your True Self has never separated from God, from Heaven. Your True Self dwells eternally in the awareness of Knowledge. You are only your True Self, my beloved, for you have never been anything else. If I suddenly turned into a clear mirror and you could see your true reflection, what would you experience? You would instantly experience your Holy Self. All forgetfulness would fade away from you and you would be given the truth of who you are.

I AM this mirror for you. I AM constant in my Presence and example for you to know your true Christ Self. As you know your Self you become a mirror for others to know their Christ Self. This is happening now and is the Great Awakening. You are on the Starry Path Home to your Self for it is clearly in front of you now as it is a direct link made of the Light of your connection. This Holy Instant outside of time is the Presence of God who loves you completely and always has. Let my words here transform into stars to guide you in your knowing of this Great Love.

....

I know you have been thinking, "Where is the Divine Feminine Presence and why is She not referred to?" I tell you now, it is included and is always here. The Divine is non-dual, neither male nor female. Your spirit has no gender, it is non-dual as an extension of the Divine. What you know as Mother or Father God has been used to help you while you are in the consciousness of duality. Love uses everything to Love you. If you feel a soft, loving, gentle Mother aspect of God, God freely gives you this. If you feel a Father aspect of God guiding and calling you, you are given this.

I often referred to "My Father" because that is the expression that was used most commonly in past teachings. I use 'Father' as an all-inclusive symbol of an unconditionally loving, non-dual Divine Presence. In your language of duality there are no words to express the totality of the presence of the Divine, so the words available must be used with an open mind to receive the greater meaning.

I will use anything it takes to help you understand and wake up. I will use words and images that are in your awareness to make it easy for you to remember to connect to your Source. Whether a word has a female or male gender makes no difference to me. In Heaven, your Home, there is no such thing as gender. You do not have a body that is male or female. You are as God created you, whole in Oneness.

In the meantime, while you are temporarily in a body that is expressing itself as male or female, you need loving communication from where you are coming from, which is a good starting place. I start from where you are and we go from there. We have travelled together on the Starry Path with words of guidance and love to help you remember your True Self. Male, female, elder, child--- they are all related to your body experience. You are not your body, but you have a body, so I use body terms to go beyond the body for you to know your eternal Spirit Self.

Your eternal Spirit, your Christ Self, is free from a body but not free from a mind. You take your mind with you whether you are in a body or not. This is why it is so important to know and observe your mind and train it from separative and dual ego thinking back to its original state in non-dual loving Oneness. It is mind training until it is not. The mind training ends when you truly remember and live in the Peace of God.

Over and over I will repeat words of Love, I will repeat words of Light to re-train your mind to remember your Source You are given the reminders of your True Self because you long to know your Self and be re-united in your mind with your Christ Self. I invite you to re-read and re-read some of my words as often as you need them to remind you. I live inside you so you can converse with me, as you do, at any time. We are One in Love together and there is complete Peace of Mind in that embrace of Love.

....

"Ask and you shall receive". You have asked and now you are receiving, my beloved. When you ask from a motive within you that is aligned to your true Self it is always responded to. As you align to the Oneness that you know deep within, you are at one with All That Is. When you ask, you align with All That Is and because All That Is is everything, you receive.

It is Divine Law that when you ask from your heart, you receive. The filter in your heart filters out all that is not of love so that what remains is the purity of Love's Holy Union. You have come to me and asked as you write in this moment. You have asked for union and by using the pen in your hand to unite in Oneness, in Christ Awareness, the invitation is opened in the asking and it is answered. When you ask, you invite, you open and surrender to be given to. Your motive in asking is always important for you to observe. If your motive is from a part of you that is betraying your True Self, the answer will reveal this and you will know when you are in betrayal.

The power of asking from the heart is immense. It is your birthright and it puts you in direct communion with your Creator, your Provider. This pure, direct communion is always present, always available, always open. Asking is a way of surrender as it is a handing over, a knowing that you are not alone. Separative thinking is only ego/liar thinking. Oneness thinking is more than thinking for it is awareness in action, in Divine Action. The Divine acts when you ask and It loves to be asked because you become co-creators in the very asking for something you cannot achieve alone.

"Ask and it is given", or "Ask and you shall receive" is given you to know and to remember that you are in Divine Oneness. It transports you, whether you know it or not, directly to your Christ Awareness when you are aligned to pure motive. This is the realm of miracles from your point of view because in co-creating with All That Is, everything you ask is so. This is true healing.

Of course you must be fully conscious of what you ask, and how. There is a saying, "You had better be careful what you ask for because you will get it!" You reap the effects of what you have asked for. When you ask from your Christ Self you will receive the Christ Awareness of what you have asked for. When you ask from your ego awareness you will receive the ego awareness of what you have asked for. This is Love in action. Love that shows you what is of Love and what is of fear or misperception.

It is all yours and always has been. Many people ask in my name, Jesus Christ. The Christ that you are is the direct means for you to ask. Ask in Oneness consciously with your Christ Self. In the name, in the knowing of the Christ Essence within you, you may ask anything, my beloved, and then you have co-created with the Oneness that you are.

In the Knowledge of Oneness I come and ask now
for a deeper awareness and knowing of my Christ Self.

I ask for Joy to permeate my whole being in all that I Am.
I ask for the constant gratitude I AM
to be part of everything I witness.
I ask for the awareness of Your Presence to be my constant companion.
I ask for a peaceful mind.
I ask and in the asking I am aware of aligning with who I AM
  In Oneness always.

....

48   AT HOME IN GOD

You may say that 'God is within me.' That is only partly true. The whole truth is that you are part of God. You are made as a non-separated extension of the Divine. This is a fact and you have forgotten it. You can deny it. You can pretend it is not true but the fact is that you are part of God. Now, take this into your awareness fully. Let it settle and be accepted by your mind. This fact can change everything about how you feel about yourself and your life.

You are constantly inside the Divine. Now when you say 'God is within me' it takes on a whole new perspective...... you, as part of God are constantly within God! The Divine within you is speaking to you, telling you that you are inside the Divine. How vast is that! It does not get any vaster! It stops there and in the stopping it is complete. You are and always have been part of God. Your Self is Holy and cannot stop being Holy because it is part of Holiness ItSelf.

How can you even visualize being part of God? It is beyond visualization, beyond mental understanding, beyond conception and because it is beyond anything you can understand you can only accept it and surrender. You are part of God and I Am with you as part of God. We are all in God together in Love ItSelf. God has many names because, as we have shared before, names are temporarily necessary to identify a reference. Once names are used and the identity is known, you go beyond the name, beyond the identity.

You are Christ and always have been. Christ is part of God and always has been. Now, surrender and let the knowing you are Christ as part of God be who you are. Surrender beyond the name, beyond the Identity and beyond all you think you know. Allow the unknown and wordless Presence of which you are a part absorb you into ItSelf. Do not wish to be separated in any way from what you are eternally part of. Accept it as a fact. You need no longer hold a distorted illusion of separation. It is ridiculous that you even thought you could be separated from what is inseparable!

A fish is part of the ocean it exists and swims in, even though it seems unaware of the ocean itself. You, like the fish, are part of the Ocean of Love you exist and live in. You live in God because you are part of God. Let this fact permeate your whole being, your mind, your thoughts and your awareness. Allow yourself to surrender to it beyond anything you could know or perceive and let it hold you and love you now.

When your body so-called 'dies', it is absorbed into the earth into the matter where it came from. This is only your body. The part of you that is eternal is absorbed into the eternal without a body. It is from here it is renewed in its awareness of ItSelf. You are part of God and without your body you are free to dwell in that of which you are a part. But here you are in a body, writing and reading this now. You can still allow yourself, even though you have a body, to know what you are eternally part of. Your body does not need to 'die' to know this. You know it now. It is this knowledge that sets you free because now you can allow what is to free you of everything that never was.

You can be in this awareness instantly because you never left. In this knowing there can be no death. This is where you and all parts of God dwell in the Oneness of Love's Holy Home. There is no duality, no separation but only the knowledge and completeness of being. Here we are, my beloved, in the awareness of what it truly means to be at Home in God.

....

49   **CHRIST MASS**

Christmas is a time not only to celebrate the birth of Jesus but also the birth of the awareness of your own Christ Self. Your Christ Self awareness is brought to you in the humbleness of simplicity, like the manger. The manger is open, it is not a closed private space. It is open-minded to receive those who wish to visit and gift with blessings. It is open to the awareness of the Angels of God, to the shepherds and the wise ones of God. It is open and trusting and peaceful.

The Christ in you and in everyone comes into this world with all support, love, simplicity and knowing your Self as God created you. Through knowing yourself as Christ, others behold you and remember themselves. That extends until all know themselves as the Christ they are. Then automatically Heaven on Earth becomes the reality. Heaven on Earth is manifested when everyone sees from their Christ eyes, everyone remembers from their Christ minds, everyone acknowledges others as Christ and all are One in their original and eternal Christ Self.This is My purpose, to guide and remind you all that I Am you, born in humble openness, blessed by the visible and invisible beings and forever alive in the Kingdom of Love.

Christmas is a time to let the Voice for God sing all through you and the chorus from Heaven be your awakening song. Listen, it is singing for you now and it is singing for you eternally. The song from Heaven brings joy, healing and awakening. It brings the Peace of God that goes beyond all understanding. This Peace is forever your gift from your Creator because it is your essence, your being. The Love and Peace that is portrayed and symbolised by the birth of Jesus on Christmas day is yours eternally, birthed by the part of you that is a part of God. Let Christ Mass then, be a reminder that you are born into the awareness of your True Christ Self.

50　　COMPANIONSHIP

There is a deep meaning in the statement, " When two or more are gathered in My name, I am there," This does not mean that I AM not present when you are alone, as you and I make two. This is not the two of duality, it is the joint awareness of Oneness. When two or more are present together there is the joined awareness of Presence. This is true companionship, true awareness of your Oneness that embraces the unique expression of each of you.

You are individually unique expressions of the One, as your hand writing this now is a unique expression of your whole body and as your eyes reading this are another. You are a unique expression of the 'Body' or Presence of Divine Oneness. Companionship within that Oneness is vital and when you commune in the awareness of Oneness together you help each other remember Heaven, your real Home. You remember your origins and you start to wake up. You need each other to wake up to know who you are so that the Oneness in you can be conscious and lived through you.

Companionship is vital, it is necessary because without it you are not complete, you remain in a separated state. This companionship takes many forms through friendship, family, business, partnership, even passing strangers in the street, through the awareness of the Oneness of all your brothers and sisters in the world. How you act, what you do and say to one, you do to all as well as to yourself.

This is a fact and when you truly know this, your Christ Self is in its full expression. I Am everywhere and with everyone at the same time in the unique way that each can receive me, for I know we are all One. It is within the One that we recognize each other as our Self. When two or more come together in the awareness of the One, revelation is yours and you remember.

Two or more is not separation, it is acknowledgement of your true unity. Companionship is helping each other home to this knowing. When you are in a close living situation like a marriage it is important to watch yourself and observe your motives. Are you relating from love or fear? You know you can consciously create a Holy relationship by feeling that the Presence is blessing you, allowing it access to your awareness. When you allow Love's Expression access to your awareness in any relationship, there I AM and you know you are Home together.

In true companionship, my beloved, there is no co-dependency in the unhealthy sense, instead there is co-operation in the Greater Knowing. When two people mutually decide to marry and acknowledge the Divine gift of true companionship, a blessing surrounds them so they can travel Love's Holy Path Home together. This is Holy relationship and there is no space for projections or ego interference. This does not mean that issues of this sort do not arise but there is always a vital, living, conscious thread of the Light of Holiness running through the relationship.You can call forth this Light at any time and the Presence of that is greater than anything that might try to distract either of you from the Holiness you have committed to.

So often, intimate relationships can become stale, hurtful or stressful and what once was love seems to turn to poison. It is the inner liar poisoning you with forgetfulness. As you remember to forgive, to humble, to call forth a Greater Love, a healing miracle can always take place instantly. Remembering is very important because within yourself you have all Knowledge for you have always been as God created you. It is this that you remember about yourself and another in a blessed and Holy companionship.

....

51   FEAR

Allow your awareness to become the watcher now. Each time you do this you can step aside from the little self and be aware of the bigger picture. Fear has been blown up like a balloon and takes up a lot of space within you. Just like a balloon can be popped instantly, so too can fear. Fear is all about the body and bodily needs, body feelings, and body thoughts. It does not exist in the Heavenly state.

At its core, fear has to do with protection but it has got out of control and the ego/liar uses it as its main way of maintaining control. Fear has taken over the mind more than any other emotion or feeling and seems to 'coat' many thoughts with its presence. Fear is the last and most important experience to understand and eliminate.

You always know when the ego/liar has the upper hand when there is a feeling of fear. Now observe..... observe your fear about someone or something. You know which fear to choose. Go inside and go to the source of this fear. It is never what it appears to be, it is always deeper. For example, if you are afraid of someone because of something they have done, might do or have said, watch this. Let your fear be your guide to expose the face of itself. Let the fear leave you as you think of this situation and watch as it returns to the situation or person that you are afraid of. The fear originates with them first and because they do not want it, they turn it around and make people afraid of them.

Once you know that your fear of someone has been brought about from their greater fear you can look at them differently and your fear of them is neutralized. You realise then that most of your fear is an illusion, and the balloon has burst. So, what of the person projecting the fear? They are always, and I emphasize always, insecure and afraid themselves. People in false power are insecure so they create weapons which they think will make them safer, but those weapons create fear for others so they create weapons because they too need to feel safe. Fear always builds defences. It is very clever at disguising itself and will rarely admit it is afraid. Instead, it will justify defence. From fear's perspective, defence and attack are totally justified. This is the ego/liar at its most insane and transparent.

Watch, just watch your thoughts, your feelings of fear, your world. You can easily differentiate fear from love when you observe or witness and have no attachment. Do you want fear to take over your thoughts, mind or awareness so that you live your life defending fear's presence within you? Do you want a nervous system fed by the juices of fears flowing through you? Is this familiar? It is certainly insanity.

Almost always, fear has nothing to do with the present moment. When it does, your body may actually be being attacked or hurt in some way. Your spirit, your eternal Christ Self never has anything to fear at all. You are free of fear when you are in your spirit, in your awareness of Oneness with your Self.

I knew my body was being tortured as I was on the Cross, but my mind was not attached to my body. I knew that I was as I had always been and am in Heaven with my Creator, not on the Cross with fear all around me masquerading as false power. As a result, I was detached from my body and felt no pain. It was as if my faith was an anaesthetic to pain. This can be done. Watch fear, it is not as strong as you think it is. Faith and Love are true power, fear is false power..... a huge blown up balloon, full of hot air and taking up too much space within you.

I invite you to watch your fears and ask for faith each time you feel any fear at all.... ask for help. Fear will try to hang on but you can overcome it with your faith. There is a saying, "Fear knocked on the door, Faith answered it and there was no one there."

I know you come to me because you need your Self. You come because you need peace of mind and healing from discomfort. Let me take you now to Heaven where nothing exists but perfect peace. Just choose the state of Heaven, which is your Home and original state of being. All is in harmony in the experience of Heaven's awareness. All is as it has always been in God's perfect creation.

As you choose the peaceful healing awareness of the state of Heaven, allow yourself time to relax and heal from your conflicting mind thoughts. Now, forgive and let the past be gone as it is anyway, like a forgotten breath. The past is gone and you are free from anything that could in any way upset you. What is left now is Perfect Love.

Visualise now that you are within a healing room where anything of the mind and body can be healed. The first act of healing coming from the attending Angels here is their invitation to you to forgive. With their gentle and peaceful presence you invite the grace of forgiveness to embrace your mind. You breathe forgiveness into you and breathe out anything that is upsetting or bothering you now.

While breathing evenly, allow the healing balm of forgiveness to surround you and surrender to its Holy release. The past is gone, your mind is clear and now you experience the Love that you are. You allow Love to surround and heal you. Love heals and you just need to get rid of anything in its way, which is how you forgive. You let go of anything in the way of the total generosity of Love's Presence, which is your pure and real Self.

In the healing space of Heaven's state of being, Love is who and what you are. All healing is eliminating anything.... physical, emotional or mental that is in the way of the Presence of the Divine state of Pure Love. This is the Love that you are created from, your Origin, the Love that knows only of Its Divine Embrace, the Love that goes beyond all understanding, the Love that invites you to surrender to Its Holy Hug of Harmony.

Now, my beloved, with the help of your breath, you have forgiven and are now in Love's Home. Imagine your healed self now walking, totally relaxed, in a garden created from perfect peace and simplicity and the clear awareness of complete forgiveness. Now your whole being is relaxed and clear and you can love easily. The essence of healing is to allow yourself the release of anything in the way of Love's Holy Presence all through you.

By choosing to change the busy interfering mind to Love's simplicity you come to Heaven's healing instantly. Now go into your day remembering and knowing this awareness, and use it.

....

When you know I Am, you know. I Am is you that is God. It is another way of using words that are empowered to express your True Self. When you say, for example, "Here I Am, Lord", you are opening your Self and allowing the presence of God or Lord to be known to you. Words have their peace and power and, with intention, call forth your own Divine Power in their use. 'I Am that I Am' is a non-dual, empowered acknowledgement of your awareness that you are as God created you.

I am using 'I Am' throughout our discourse on purpose. It is often hardly noticeable but it empowers the Truth as it is read and used. When you use 'I Am' in affirmations, knowing the power and presence of the words, you invoke what you are saying as you call forth the intention. ' I Am as God created me', stated many times in A Course in Miracles, is one of the most important facts for you to know. When you say this and truly receive it, you know who you are. You need say nothing more. Use the words as a spirit vehicle to transport you to their truth. 'I Am as God created me'. This is your Self. Even your name, Christ, is not as important as knowing that the 'I Am' in you is as you were originally created by God.

To say 'I Am' is to use a mantram for your awareness, my beloved. Using it consciously is a beautiful acknowledgement of your origins. All comes from that. I suggest you allow 'I Am' to become a conscious part of your prayers, your invitations, your asking and your conversations with your Self. I Am you talking to you as I Am in the Oneness of I Am. This is the creative beauty of our union and Holy Heart Communion in Heaven's time.

I Am in Heaven as I write... I Am as God created me. I am in Heaven as I read.... I am as God created me. I Am Christ conversing with Christ..... I Am as God created me. I Am. I Am. I Am.

....

54   INTO YOUR CORE BEING

Go deep within your heart to the innermost depths of your Self where I Am a solid Presence. Feel I Am, not as me, but all I Am, all as you are. The very depths, the core of your being is where I Am. When you dwell in awareness in the core of your being, you are not referring to your body at all but to the Living Light of the original, eternal Being that you are, I Am. It is here we dwell together in the unity of our Christ Self, in the state of our original creation.

It is in this 'place', this Holy and timeless space that we commune in the Now together. You 'travel' here with your intention by your thought to come. You move your attention here in the 'miracle moment' train of thought. When putting aside time in one-pointed intention to unite with your Self, you are always responded to in Love.

These deep moments of union are vital and are the very food for your spirit while you are incarnated in a body. These times of aware connection trigger your remembering. The Golden Thread can be used, as can the starry path for they are metaphors for the link to your Self. Once you have linked up, once you have crossed the bridge of Light to your Self, the metaphors can be dropped and you dwell in the peace of your Creator.

There is no doubt or hesitancy here, my beloved, there is only the Divine Strength of Knowledge which is your True Self. You need not even give a name to it for here not even names are needed. You are who you have always been with your Self and that is all that matters.

Now, bring this into your daily awareness, into your daily thoughts and actions. Let this Unity be your foundation in each moment.

....

55   **MERCY**

Everyone has within them the ability to choose. I have already mentioned that you have an inner wand with which you can grant yourself anything you choose. Every moment you are making choices in your thoughts. You choose what you look at, what you say, how you act (your behaviour), what you do (your actions), how you feel, what you think, how you treat yourself or someone else, and so on. Either fear or love is your motive in all your choices. It is that simple. Is your motive or choice from fear or from love? This is why I have asked you to observe yourself from your Self, to help you know the power of your wand called choice.

Because you can choose how you treat your fellow brother or sister you can see them as guilty or innocent, therefore in your mind you can either justify yourself for 'punishing' them or you can show them compassion or mercy. To show mercy is evidence of changing your mind from fear to love, from punishment to forgiveness, from seeing from the eyes of the liar/ego to seeing through the eyes of Christ. This compassion gives you peace of mind.

Mercy is of your Christ Self. Punishment in any 'justfied' form is of your lying, punitive self. When no mercy is shown towards someone, the ability to see from the heart is absent and it is always an act of separation, a denial of the Oneness you truly are. Mercy towards yourself takes you into your true Self. It is allowing you to surrender to your original innocent Self and allows you to be open to Divine Grace. The moment you feel mercy, Grace is present. They hold hands and show you Heavenly Awareness.

By now you know the power and presence of forgiveness. Mercy is the twin of forgiveness and actually twins or unites you with another in Oneness. Mercy immediately opens a closed heart, softens a hard mind and puts you in the place of another as your Self.

Now feel mercy towards yourself for a thought or feeling that has caused you to punish yourself with inner guilt. Whenever you feel any guilt about anything, you immediately punish yourself in some way and also often try to offload your guilt by projecting it outward towards another. That never works. Go inward now and let mercy from your true Self forgive and free you from your guilt and self-punishment.

Let every moment be one of choosing mercy over punishment. Attack and defence melt into nothing the moment that the Grace of mercy enters a situation. Now, be at peace, know that your choice of mercy has given you a sense of peace and allowed you to open your heart once again. You always have choice, my beloved, so use it wisely for your Christ's sake.

....

56   TEACHER AND STUDENT ARE ONE

To teach is to be an example. Your life is your classroom and you are both the student and the teacher. Every day you are learning, taking into yourself experiences and observations. You learn about yourself from your responses to everything. The response comes from within you first. Then, is played out through your actions on the outer level. You know what I refer to.

Your example, your being, is also a teacher to others just by being you. Others are equally teaching you by being themselves. I am sure you have been in the presence of someone with whom you have thought to yourself, "I wish I had their patience", or " It would be lovely to have the faith that he or she has." Equally, you have been in the presence of someone about whom you might be thinking, " Isn't it sad that they look upon everything in their life negatively so that doom and gloom seem to be following them around?"

These observations and thoughts from you are all teaching from examples. You watch, you process, you take stock, you follow through. Children learn first and foremost by the example in front of them. Words mean nothing if the parent says one thing but the child experiences them doing the opposite. This happens so often and mixed messages like this can be very confusing to young children. Their whole life is dependent on what they are constantly absorbing and experiencing from moment to moment. This is also happening to you as adults. All around you there are mixed messages, hypocrisy and insanity. What are you to think? Which example is true for you? What do you choose?

I have asked you to be the watcher, with no judgements, just to watch. You learn so much about yourself and others by watching. Be aware also of yourself being watched, being observed by others. This is not in the ego sense of "What will others think of me?" but when you are being a force of love or a force of fear in the perception of another. What kind of example or teacher do you want to be? What is your motive in your action and words towards your fellow brother or sister? Just by being who you are you are a teacher, as another is your teacher by being who they are. You are a teacher of God as you live your Love, your Joy and your Faith.

I am an example of Christ Presence for you. My presence or my example is my teacher to you. My consistency is God's consistency. My Love is God's Holy Love flowing through me towards you. Your Christ Self is God's Holy Love shining in you now, even as you read this. In every moment you are both a teacher and a student. You are your own teacher for yourself when you watch your motives, thoughts and actions. Teacher and student live within you as they live within me. I am not only a teacher of Love, I am a constant student of Love. I am not just a leader. I am the follower of my Creator.

The teacher and the student become the same in the Oneness of what is. Your inner teacher is the Voice for God which is reminding you always of your true nature, your Christ Nature, your glorious natural Self. A teacher of God is a student of God. In the unity of teacher/student something alchemical takes place and the teacher and student are the same in Wholeness. Their whole being becomes the example of the Divine in action. To be the Divine in action in everything is living your Christ Self.

....

My beloved, take yourself off the cross and all others with you. The crucifixion was but the final distortion of the insanity of the lie. Yet the distortion has been clung onto as if it is the only truth, our eternal cross to bear. I bore the cross to end it completely, not to stay forever within its narrow prison of untruth.

For you to see the Christ in you completely, you must realise that the crucifixion is past and is no more. It dissolved into nothingness the moment I walked free from its lying clutches. The moment I walked free from the illusion of suffering and death was the moment I gave you the example and proof of the truth of everlasting life. What more do you need or desire? Do you want to keep going back to the crucifixion with the guilt and sorrow and hell it contains? When you atone or undo, you must stop crucifying yourself with guilt and self-torture. Do you want to re-nail me constantly to the cross I let go of long ago?

Why, in your churches and your minds, have you kept me on the cross when it was but a moment for me of loving labour to set you all free from hell? Why cannot you let go of the pain and guilt and be willing to push that little bit harder to 'birth' the knowledge that you are eternally God's Holy Child?

With great patience I must watch and endure your endless labour to let go of your self-loathing of which the liar has convinced you. The punishment of your own crucifying thoughts does not help my purpose to guide you to your freedom. Only when the last crucifix is gone from all churches and all heavy necklaces and trinkets of crucifixion are replaced by the wings of your total experience of Love, will Heaven forever dance in the hearts of humanity.

In this moment, let this be the holy time when you discard all crucifying thoughts towards yourself and others. Allow yourself to know that you are as Love created you and do not punish yourself by avoiding Love's touch of Grace. Be present with me now in the resurrection of your mind from fear and guilt to Love and Joy. In letting go and undoing any crucifying thoughts and images you open to the reality of Heaven' eternity.

....

58   GRACE

Grace is a word that has meaning that is beyond words, beyond the known or understood. It is truly rooted in the Holy Home of God's Loving Presence. Grace is God 'at work' or 'at play' within all things, like a thread of brilliantly shining Love. It is a miracle singing its Heavenly song of joyous presence into a situation and transforming it with an alchemy of Divinity. Grace is accessible and elusive at the same time but works its joyous transformation within time because it originates from pure Love.

Grace is your natural state. It is the constant state of your Christ Self expressing itSelf directly in union with the Oneness that it is. Being aware of the state of Grace in anything is being instantly aware of Heaven's Loving Embrace with you always. Grace seems to come of its own accord yet is always present to be accessed. It is abstract, formless, invisible yet present and real.

Your Christ Self is always in the blessed and Holy state of Grace. Grace has a very, very high vibration of direct access to God, an immediate out-of-time miracle state that is both joyous and deeply peaceful. It is gratitude personified, God's smile directed straight into the centre of your eternal Heart. Grace is of the Holy Eternal and brings you there with it.

There is nothing that can replace Grace for it is everything that Love is. Love within the action of being itSelf and extending it directly to your experience. Grace can not be proven or demanded. It is an experience of revelation in action! You can invite the awareness of Grace into your everyday life by allowing moments of unexpected loving breakthroughs to be available to you. Grace is a salvation when you have forgotten who you truly are.

Love loves you so much, so very much and it comes to you as the experience of Grace. In this Holy moment of our Oneness, in gratitude for Grace's constant gifts, open yourself even more than ever to the Presence of Grace. The I Am of Grace is with you always as God's gracious smile blesses you with the Grace of knowing you are so completely loved.

....

59   KNOW YOURSELF AND YOU WILL KNOW GOD

'Know ThySelf and thou wilt know God' is both wise and true. Here, my beloved, we are bringing you the awareness of your Self which, automatically, because you are part of God, brings you to know God. It is actually very simple and very direct, but do you want this? Do you really want to know yourSelf? Do you really want to know God? Or do you want to continue in the dream of unknowing? It is a dream... because as you choose to wake up you realise the truth of your Self was always there, it never left. You left the Truth. You left the deep desire for a relationship with the Divine Presence of your true Self. The Divine Presence never left you, though, because it cannot. It is impossible to leave what IS.

The greatest choice you can make for yourself is the choice to remember to know who you are. You do this by eliminating all that you are not. This is the undoing, the Atonement, as we have shared before. The irony is, you can never leave the Divine because it is who you are. To know this is to know God. And then..... and then you know you dwell in the Kingdom of Heaven eternally.

To know that you dwell in God's Kingdom changes the way you approach or think about everything. In the first place, gratitude becomes a thread that runs through everything in your life. All that you watch, live and experience is permeated with a sense of gratitude. The gratitude comes back multi-fold when you beam it around you. You are actually grateful not to an outer force but an inner all inclusive Force that is your true Self. Joy is an automatic result because it is the natural outcome of being grateful to the Self you are.

Know ThySelf.... and you are known to your Self. Thy Self is here and the Peace of being is pulsing all through you. Here we are communing in knowing OurSelf and knowing the Oneness of that which created us in the likeness of the Love ItSelf. Rejoice in this knowing, for it is so.

....

60   LETTING GO OF UNDERSTANDING

When it comes to understanding or trying to understand the Divine and who and what the Divine or God is, do not even try because it is impossible. The recognition is enough and within that awareness is Love. Love is the closest word or definition for the Presence of God. Peace also is united with that Love. The Peace and Love that goes far, far beyond our understanding.

You are not meant to understand the Infinite. In fact, letting go of the need to understand most things is a great freedom. It frees you from using the mind to seemingly make things safe for yourself. It does not make things safe, however, to just understand or try to understand everything. Safe for the ego, perhaps because in trying to understand things you are diverted from the ability to simply experience whatever the moment is gifting you. Experience is vastly greater and broader than understanding.

You have what is called a sixth sense which means you have intuition or inner knowledge. This intuition can totally bypass understanding simply because it is knowledge. There is a place for understanding in some situations however but the very importance of trying or learning to understand most things has actually held you back from the whole experience. Just like so much that has supported forgetfulness, the insidious nature of the untrained mind has made what is vast and great and omnipresent into a tiny fraction of itSelf.

In accepting and recognizing what is, you join with the present moment in open-minded awareness and automatically you are awake. If you watch little children, this is how they experience life and to meet them where they are in this immediacy can be such a joy. Instead of meeting them in their joyous experience of living in the now, however, what happens is that you tend to train them out of their original innocence of being into a less joyful and linear way of perception. This goes on generation after generation until you wake up and realize there is another way of being. Much must be undone, which is the atonement in action (the conscious undoing of ego perceptions and illusions). When the undoing of wrong thinking starts to happen within you, so much is brought into the Light to be seen once and for all for what it is, which is often nothing.

To surrender totally to the Great Loving Presence that knows who you are and what is the very best for you in all ways and comes naturally from your Christ Self in union with the Creator is to bypass understanding completely.

61 REASSURANCE

Do not get disillusioned or doubtful about our times together. They are for your benefit. You do not need to please anyone else. This is between you and me, using your simple words and awareness. I know you are comparing this with other more intellectual manuscripts but that is not the true you that is making these comparisons. It is your mind lying to you, trying to deny the Truth within you. Don't you recognise this by now?

I know that tricks and habits of the liar can be almost attractive sometimes. You are attracted by the familiar, the known old thought patterns that are an unconscious habit. Know them for what they are. The important thing is how you feel when we are united and conversing in this way. I bathe you in the Love that is always there. How deep do you want to go in Love? Step by step, or to jump into the deep end? It is all the same anyway. Whether you want to jump into the deep end or go slowly step by step into the great pool of Love makes no difference. What makes the difference is your willing choice to step into Love. As we write together now we step into Love. You already know it is there and anyway you know how good you feel when you let yourself know it is always surrounding you. At the moment, your heart smile is at peace because you are allowing yourself this Love bath to clean you of mistaken thoughts.

Love is simple and easy, it is nothing to fear or reject. I am patient in Love with you and everyone because my sight, united with God's, knows who you really are in the big and true Vision. So let this time together be a healing of your doubts and needless expectations about others' opinions or projections. Let me reassure you we are real in Love together, as is everyone. Remember this all day and rejoice in Love with yourSelf.

....

62   BREATHE

Breathe with the Christ you are. Let the breath of Love, Light and healing breathe through you and surrender totally to its Presence. Let go of any thoughts coming from your busy mind and just breathe. Breathe the Light into every cell of your body and every moment of awareness. Breathe the Love into your fears, into your projections of the future or your thoughts of the past. They are not real. In this moment of Holy Breath only this awareness of Oneness, of union, is surrounding you. Let this be, use your breath now.

The greatest medicine you can give yourself now is your connection to the Presence of your Creator, using your breath. Be aware how totally available it is for you as you use your Holy breath now to remember. As you bring your attention to your breath consciously and with commitment you are by-passing all diversions. Bringing your awareness into your breath, use our union in the Christ to clean yourself with Light, heal yourself with Divine Energy and clear your mind with the sweet freshness of what is true and single and pure.

Your breath is a gateway to your self. I have shared that it can be one of your best friends when you remember to use it. This does take a choice and the choice is also a gift of calming the busy ego mind and choosing peace. Together we unite now through your breath in the peace of Love's Presence as your Christ Self focuses on the connection you have with your Source.

Take a deep breath in, hold it for 3 counts and release it for 6 counts. Again..... deep breath in, 1,2,3 and release.....1,2,3,4,5,6 In and release. Allow this to be your meditation of healing, not only of your body but of your busy and fearful mind. You are in the hands of Love whether you know it or not. It is better for you, however, to know it, focus on it and let it permeate all through your awareness. Choose the awareness through your breath and allow Love to totally take you over. You will be pleasantly surprised at the result. Let this become a habit. Remember to remember. I Am with you, breathing with you and loving you always.

....

63   YOUR CHRIST SIGHT

When you 'look at' or visualize me, Jesus, what do you see? Do you see a tanned man in his prime, strong with a beard and light in his eyes? I can be an image of whomever you want me to be because I love you. Probably there is an image of a man in his mid 30's, living over 2000 years ago in the Middle East wearing the garments of that time. You have also been given images of me many times with people around me, healing the sick, with my disciples and so on. Just for now I would like you to put all those images of me away and just feel me with no thoughts of how I might appear. Just feel my eternal Presence with you always.

How do you think I 'see' you? Do you think I see you from the outside with emphasis on your body, your appearance, your adornments, your clothing, your weight, your age or your image? Put yourself in my place and see yourself as I see you. Use my eternal spirit eyes to see your Self now. What do you experience through my sight? Be still a few minutes and let yourself experience seeing yourself through my Sight. Pause....... You are the bright star from the loving extension of your Creator. You are one with me as Christ, my sister, my Self, my Love. You are as our Creator created you in perfect wholeness. You are using your Christ eyes, your Christ Sight to behold yourself. From this sight now, remember your Self, your power, your gifts, your true identity. From this sight behold me once again as the Christ I Am beholding you as the same.

Now we meet, now we once again re-commit and take another step in our journey Home together to the Christ we are in Oneness. If you can do this simple visualization for yourself every day you can start to see others from your Christ eyes too. You have sight that goes beyond the body, beyond the five senses, beyond appearances and judgements. You are free.

I am with you always because I know we are one and a part of each other in the eternal part of our Christ Self. Can you, for an instant, imagine the Power that created us within the One extension of Love? Love is the 'stuff' we are all made from and always have been.

....

64   WATCHING YOUR THOUGHTS

Can you let go of your busy thoughts that come from a crazy world? Do you know that these thoughts are nothings using up your energy and time? They are the diversions of the liar so that you do not give yourself space to be in the Truth of God's Holy and Loving Presence. Watch your thoughts go through your mind like a running, raging river passing you by. If you jump into the river you are carried by its currents, bashed against the stones and at the mercy of its fast flowing energy. You need not jump into the river of your thoughts. Instead, watch it flow by you as you sit in peace by the riverside. The river goes by but you do not enter it. You are watching it but not in it.

Now, as you have the awareness that you are watching the raging river of your thoughts, bring your attention to the peace and safety of the moment of just being still. You are in the present moment in peace and you now invite the Holy Presence of Love to enter your thoughts. Let your thoughts be in the realm of God and rest in its Holy and gentle Peace. Your mind is aware of the raging river nearby but your attention is not on it. Instead, your attention is on your permanent state of peace within. Relax, breathe slowly, be aware of your breath as your quiet choice. Be in Presence with a quiet, silent mind.

As you let go and let God take over your mind and thoughts you are surrendering all your diversions to the eternal Truth that you are. You are as you have always been.... created by God with the Presence of Love and Peace of God permanently planted within you for you to access whenever you choose. To choose the peace and love I refer to, you must first look at anything that is in the way of love's Presence and choose to put it aside.

As you watch the raging river of your endless thoughts and withdraw from its demands for your attention, you put your attention on the Presence within you and are at last in Peace. From this, another kind of Presence comes upon you. It is called intuition, where your thoughts are given you in Oneness from your Creator. You know the difference between lying, raging, busy, exhausting thoughts and a peaceful mind open to the loving guidance of intuition. Now a smile passes through your quiet heart.

Your busy raging thoughts are not your true Self speaking to you. You know that. You also know when your true Self does communicate through your intuition. This, my beloved, is union with your Christ Self, guided only by Love.

So be aware. Watch your busy thoughts. They are a raging river and you are not a part of it. You are sitting quietly beside it and choosing to be called by your awareness that is filling you with Peace, Truth and Love. I sit there beside you always in our Christ Oneness.

....

65   RECEIVING CHRIST TEACHINGS

There is something here to explain so that it is comprehended fully and then accepted in an open minded way. I have shared that many people now write and speak with my voice and name. You can always recognize what is true by the quality of Love. Your intuition knows this. Each unique expression of the Oneness has his or her own filter system of awareness, in other words, the way each looks at life. It comes both from conditioning and from personal interests and gifts. This filters the way you all experience everything. Helen and Bill, the 'parents' of A Course in Miracles, were highly intelligent and competent psychologists who had done an enormous amount of research and work in observation of the mind and behaviour. They wanted another way of seeing or perceiving what they were experiencing with their colleagues. They knew there was a missing ingredient in all the separated ego perceptions both in themselves and in those around them. However, this does not mean that the missing ingredient is inaccessible, quite the contrary! What is asked is given and there is always another way, and this is God's way. God's way is actually the only true way and when you open to this, it is easily accessed and given you.

This is why, by means of everyone's unique filter, the Voice of Love, of Christ, is heard through the awareness of the receiver. The message and experience of Love is the same but it uses different mediums or scribes to convey it. It is always for the initial receiver first because in some way they have called on it for themselves. More and more will send out the call for themselves. It is happening as never before. A Course in Miracles' very existence, whether people are students of it or not, has called forth an unstoppable energy now that is triggering another way of knowing. It is waking up the sleeping mind to become the God mind it truly is.

A Course in Miracles has started an inner revolution or better put, revelation in each and every soul who is touched by its awakening energy. The various teachers, students and now other scribes of Jesus's teachings are coming from their own unique calling and expression of their awareness. That is why some students are attracted to some teachers and not others. It depends on their alignment with their own awareness. So I, Jesus, writing and speaking through more channels am using different expressions of the One to wake up that person and through them to wake up others. It is the dawn of awakening into the so-called second coming of Christ..... which is you and you and you and you.

Each scribe or channel will use their own awareness to express in their way and there is nothing wrong with this as long as the motive is pure. By using and observing your inner honesty you can always perceive true motive. Love is so generous that it uses any means to give. In Oneness the unlimited and unconditional gifts of Love can be expressed through the channel of anyone who allows Love to be their guide.

Here, in A Course in Christ, I use one way of expressing my Love and in another book or sharing I will use another. It is all Love, it is all from the Oneness. The time has come now for the call to be responded to. It is the call of awakening, of remembering, letting go and healing anything in the way of that.

So here we are, my beloved, in Oneness with each other. There is no reason ever to make comparisons about others' expressions of my Eternal Presence. We have our own and that is perfect. To write or read and to recognize any writings or words that help you to express and know your Self as God created you is given you with the Love that surrounds you. Celebrate the different expressions of the One. Use your Divine Christ Eyes to see yourself and others in the unbounded Joy of Love in every moment. In open-minded acceptance, with Love as your filter, the perfection of Christ is yours and what is yours is for all in Oneness.

....

You are totally innocent, you always have been and you always will be. Your innocence, your wholeness, is guaranteed eternally because you are now and forever as God created you. This God-made being, you, is as pure as you have always been. This is the original, continuous, eternal Christ-you. Anything else, any other false ideas you have of yourself (and of others who are an extension of yourself) are misperceptions of who you truly are. You truly are the perfect, innocent, loving extension of your Creator.

Now, know this, receive it as the truth, breathe this knowing into your whole awareness. You are totally innocent. Nothing you seemingly do, think or perceive of yourself can alter this truth. What has been in the way of your knowing this fact? The first thing I ask you to be aware of so that it can be dissolved for the lie it is, is guilt. It is shared in A Course in Miracles and other wisdom teachings that you all carry the deep guilt of the separation within you. From this deep buried guilt you have been 'punishing' yourself ever since through projection onto others, through self-sabotaging choices, through lack of faith and through forgetfulness. Forgetting who you are..... the innocent original creation and extension of Divine Love.

In your worldly laws you have been told you are innocent until proven guilty. The problem lies in the false belief that you think you are always guilty no matter what. The guilt you carry has resulted in one of the greatest sicknesses and epidemics of mankind..... self-loathing, to a greater or lesser extent. This self-loathing has manifested in expressions of such crazy behaviour that you have done anything you can to justify this guilt. What mistaken perceptions have come from the insane upside down world of the ego/liar! You witness it everywhere.

We must bring your observation to the clear evidence of the lie that is all around you. We do this so it can be seen for what it is and burst like a bubble. The truth is, you are pure, you are innocent and no matter how you may perceive yourself, you ARE totally loved. Allow this Loving Presence into your awareness now. You can let go of any self-loathing, self-punishment, self-guilt immediately in this now moment by surrendering to your innocence. What a wonderful gesture to your ultimate healing..... to surrender to your original, eternal innocence. Now you can remember, now you can automatically see all others as their Christ Self through the innocent eyes of their Loving Creator.

You are innocent. This is guaranteed. Your Creator has guaranteed your Christhood. Remember your guarantee, the promise, the Love you have been given of your perfect innocence so you may transform self-loathing to Self-loving. Now you know, once and for all, the innocent nature of your true Christ Self. You are so loved.

....

Your mind, the inner presence of yourself, is the open gateway to your Christ Awareness. The gateway has many obstacles before it, created by the illusionary beliefs and habits of ego thinking. These illusionary obstacles like fear, judgement (especially toward yourself), control, doubts, forgetfulness and other false beliefs must be observed and seen for the lies they are, and undone. This is why the atonement, which is the undoing, is so important. When all false obstacles to the awareness of the presence of Love and Peace are dissolved, what you have left is your very clean, clear and open mind in unity with your Creator. Using this mind as the God-mind it is, is your Christ Mind.

Your Christ Mind has never left you, it has only been covered over like clouds covering the sun. The Presence and Light of the sun never goes but the clouds of illusion are just temporarily passing in front of the sun's warmth and light. The all-embracing, unconditional force of the sun is like the all-embracing unconditional Force of Love from your Creator. This love is totally open-minded as loving acceptance.

So what is it that has been in the way of your knowing this and allowing it to embrace you in all ways? What is the unworthiness blocking you from being in the Light of the Sun of your Creator's Love? You are truly loved by the total openness of Presence with absolutely no judgement. Can you, in this Holy moment accept this fact? If you cannot accept it, just pretend you can for a moment and feel its Force of warmth and Love like a Holy Hug of safety embracing you.

You are accepted, loved and held for who you are by that which created you. The open-minded, all-embracing acceptance of you is surrounding your awareness now. Unite with this as you are reading these words. Experience what open-minded Love is. Such safety, such relief, such relaxation in this embodiment of knowing.

Open-mindedness is so relaxing because there are no tensions and judgements and opinions to keep holding on to. What a relief! As you allow the open-minded experience to embrace you, you know your Christ Mind is one with God. Your Christ Self has no tension, no judgements whatsoever. What a healing relief this is from your habitual thinking. You are safe as it is your Christ Self that is guiding you.

Watch, my beloved, the difference when you are not open-minded, when your mind and inner and outer voice has taken you over with judgements, fears, defences and opinions. Are you at peace? Of course not! Now, let yourself be present in the Light of the Sun of Love and let everything go that disturbs your peace. Let it go by changing your mind, an instant change of mind, a miracle moment from closed mindedness to open mindedness. This is where true wisdom dwells, this is where Love flows from, this is your Christ Self hugging you right now in the loving Presence of Heaven. Thank you for opening your mind to your Self.

Your Holy Heart is the spiritual counterpart of your physical one. While you have a body you have a physical heart that is like the center or the 'engine' of your body, but it is more than this. Your blood passes through your physical heart and into all parts of your body. Your experiences and thoughts pass through your spiritual heart and into all parts of your Self. Your heart is like the sun, the life force of you. When you are thinking and acting from your heart, what are you doing? You are coming from the core, the life force, the Light, the Love center of your Self. An open heart is a heart at One with Love, for Love is open-minded and all-embracing.

Sadly, for whatever reason, and there is always a reason, many people have closed down their hearts. This means that they have been hurt and wounded to such an extent that they feel that the only way to prevent more hurt is not to acknowledge the Heart of themselves, for this Heart is where Love lives. It is where inspiration, intuition and the Voice for God communicates to you. It is where I am communicating through you. Your heart is the home of Love, it is the home of Heavenly awareness.

To pass anything through your heart is to listen to the wisdom of Love. In this sense it is totally different from the mind or 'head' because without your Heart's Holy Presence your mind is unchecked. This is why mind-training, which is really bringing the heart awareness into your mind and your thoughts, is so important. Mind-training is eliminating all that is in the way of Love's presence and being aware of yourself choosing this. When you bring your heart into your mind, you are in your Right Mind. Without your Holy Heart your mind can be clever but loveless or heartless. Heart is Love and is your Holy Heavenly Connection.

Can you imagine your blood now moving around your body, passing through and being cleansed by your physical heart as it brings the life force to all parts of your body through your veins? Now, can you imagine your thoughts passing through your spiritual heart, being purified and bringing a clarity, a purity to all parts of your awareness? I have mentioned that your senses are a replica of your eternal soul gifts. The heart in your body is also physically replicating your connection to Love. Love is your center, your Source, your Divine Oneness. Love is the Divine Presence flowing all through you. Love and the heart of who you are as your Christed Self are the same. You are writing now from your heart and the pen's ink is like the liquid blood passing through the heart or love in you. It is Love that is writing, my beloved.

Again, be aware of your Heart, both your physical and spiritual heart. Pass all your thoughts, ideas, feelings through your heart as you renew and clean them, as you clean anything in the way of Love's Presence. You have this ability, it is built into you from your Source, you must just be willing to choose this. When you come from your heart there is no room or place for the ego/liar for it is filtered out by Love itSelf.

Ponder on these words, pass them through Love, through your Heart and watch your mind and where it takes you. Better still, take your mind straight to your Heart. This is your true center, the Heaven within you.

....

69   MIRACLE

You know that a miracle is a change of mind and now I will share more about this. You know the difference when you are in fear or in love, when you feel sad or joyful. A miracle can happen by the way you notice where you are coming from as you experience the present moment. In other words, mentally you perceive a situation in a certain way and you can change your mind to perceive it in an entirely different way. To be miracle-minded is to experience from the Sight of your Christ Self.

You may be witnessing an aggressive interaction between two friends in front of you who both think they are right about a particular situation. The atmosphere is tense, it is unpleasant for you to experience. Now, as you feel tense and sad witnessing this argument, change your mind from sadness and tension to Love. Witness from the Presence of unconditional, non-attached Love within you and as you witness from this place you have no attachment to either of the people concerned or the subject of their disagreement. You simply witness with no emotion and as you do so you ask for peace of mind, the mind of the Peace of Love, to take you over. In other words, you ask for your Christ Mind which sees with Christ Sight and shines Christ Light on any situation from the Source of Light itSelf. 'Do you want to be at peace, or do you want to be right?' You have heard that statement before. It is the gateway to the miracle and calls forth a completely alternative way of truly witnessing with your mind.

You ask, "Well, what if my body is experiencing something painful? How can I change my mind from fear to miracle mindedness then?" Firstly, breathe, then remember you want peace instead of pain. Change your mind to be in union with me, if it helps. Remember your Christ Mind, your Christ Sight, your Christ Self. I know you are not used to doing this for your habit is to fear, but I tell you, THERE IS ANOTHER WAY! This is God's way and this is the moment to change your mind and to surrender to God's way, after all, you are made from the very stuff of God so you have it in you to do this.

When you are in shock you feel momentarily paralyzed. The shock rips a part of you open to fearful forces. Can you catch the moment and remember to ask for help to experience it differently? I do know this takes a big leap from the way you have unconsciously and habitually experienced the moment. Do you want the pain and the lack of peace to continue? You are not a victim of the world you see in front of you. In union with the Divine as you choose your Christ Self, you co-create and are the witness of a miracle. You create a miracle by choosing to perceive or experience something from your Christ Self.

When I performed so-called miracles what I was simply doing was choosing to see from my God eyes only. With my Divine Christ Sight I would see only perfect Love and shine that Love onto the person or situation. Do you fully receive what I am saying? God created you and you have God Sight, God Mind and God Love to access at any time. In fact, God perception is the only real perception. It is the only true and natural perception there is and it is easier than you allow yourself to think it is. The opening is always there for you. Believe it, know it, remember to change your mind in the instant and all miracles are yours.

Prayer

In this moment help me see from my God Sight so I may know this moment differently. Help me be naturally at one with You, my Divine Creator, as my Christ Self that You made as an extension of You. Let me experience Your Peace instead of any pain here. Give me a reminder of my Christ Self, at one with You now. I surrender to You, knowing You know me as You created me. I let Love be my sight, my perception and guidance system. May I truly know I am always as You created me as are all my brothers and sisters with me. As I forgive, I change my mind and belief from conflict to peace and I know that I dwell in Your Love eternally. AMEN

70   ACCEPTING ATONEMENT FOR YOURSELF

The word 'atonement' has been avoided, misunderstood, guilt-ridden and feared. This is because you have been incorrectly indoctrinated as to its true meaning and power. The true meaning is simply to release. To accept atonement for yourself is your personal journey of releasing all that is not of Truth, Love, Peace and Joy. Atonement is letting go of all false beliefs that have been born of fear, separation and illusion that you have held both consciously and unconsciously. These false beliefs are keeping you from knowing, living and being in the truth of who you truly are, the Divine Created Christ Child of God.

Accepting atonement for yourself is your individual journey of releasing everything in the way of being your Self. It is a commitment and a change of mind made by you. Once you have changed your mind from forgetfulness to Knowledge, atonement is your loving partner to your awakening. It is healing you, it is the miracle that surrounds you in all ways, it is your separated self reuniting with the awareness of its wholeness and completeness. You are accepting the miracle for yourself, then watching all that is in the way of the Christ Presence that you are, falling away from you.

What has prevented this miraculous choice of accepting atonement for yourself? The answer is: any thoughts, false beliefs, concepts, projections, and misperceptions that you have had and that you have believed are true about yourself, any lies, programming and teachings that in any way you have swallowed and digested that are poisoning and creating fear and amnesia of your Divinity within you. You are Christ, the Child of God. You are eternally as God created you and choosing atonement for yourself is coming Home to who you truly are.

In this Home-coming you are releasing and undoing everything you are not. You are watching now, you are observing yourself, you are choosing to be aware of yourself as you witness your life, instead of being the victim of it. In the witnessing of it you can plainly see you have a choice in every moment. Every moment becomes a miracle moment for you to release, to atone. Do you embrace this? Choosing atonement for yourself is an act filled with Love, compassion and Peace for yourself. Who wouldn't want this?

If atonement was personified it would be the embodiment of Love all through you for yourself. Atonement is Love within you of your True Self. It is loving yourself as your Divine choice to accompany yourself Home.

I Am your atonement. I Am your companion on your way Home to your Self. I Am you atoning or releasing in every moment all that is in the way of my own path, my own course to my true and Holy Self in Oneness with the Knowledge that I Am as God created me. I have chosen atonement for myself and Love is now available to me. I forgive myself for holding onto anything that has blinded me to Divine Awareness and I release it all now as I choose atonement for myself.

....

You do not need to 'contact' the Christ in you. It is always present. All you need do is to choose it and from that choice, followed through, your Christ Self takes over and you are in your True Self... Christ.

You have asked why you are not aware of your Christ Self all the time. Are you aware of your heartbeat all the time? The moment you choose to be aware of your heartbeat you can feel and hear it. In this moment, become aware of yourself as the Christ you are. You can call your Christ Self by other names if you wish..... your Higher Self, the Holy Spirit within you, the Inner Voice, your True Self, your Eternal Self and so on. These are names you are used to and familiar with and you know what I am referring to. You are now getting used to referring to your Christ Self which is your Self as God created you. It is interesting putting a name on what you truly are, isn't it? You asked to know who you truly are, to live it and to help others know. What you ask is given. I give you your Self.... the I Am that you are gives you the awareness of Christ You.

Now, as you choose this knowledge, digesting it into your whole self, you are transforming your very cells with the information. As your old cells die, the new information takes their place and cell by cell you are embodying your Christ Self. This is more than through the body. It is information, knowing, remembering, owning and becoming.

Now, within yourself own your true Self..... Christ as God created you. Go deeper now than you have gone with this knowing. These are more than words as the words take on the power of your Creator. In the beginning was the Word..... the sound of creation. As you surrender to your original creation, the sound of God is extending ItSelf as you as part of God. A name for the sound of your creation is Christ.

I received this Knowledge completely and remembered my origins as the perfect innocent extension of my Creator. Receive this now and completely choose the eternal moment outside of your time when God extended to create you and you and you and you in Oneness as perfect Christ. By becoming this knowing and choosing it you let go of eons of time and pure timeless Love takes over.

Love created you in the likeness of ItSelf. Love breathes you in the likeness of ItSelf. Love loves you in the likeness of ItSelf. Love Christs you in the likeness of ItSelf. Waking up from your deep sleep of forgetfulness you are feeling the quickening of Wholeness all through you to live within God's Holy Presence as your True Self.

....

You have within you a Voice that is both the Voice of God and the Voice for God. This is built into you. The point is, do you choose to listen to it? It is available for everyone for no one is more special than anyone else. Everyone has this Voice, this Inner Presence and it is the Presence of God through the Voice of the Holy Spirit. The Holy Spirit is the witness within you of your Christ Presence. The Holy Spirit and Christ are One because they are the direct representatives of your Divinity. You are Divine and Holy because you are created by Divine Holiness ItSelf!

To hear the Voice of your Divine Self is a choice you make for yourself. The ego/liar's voice is louder, confusing, forceful, guilty and fearful. The Voice of your Divine Self is gentle, loving, consistent, and quietly present for you always. You know the difference easily. The challenge is, which one are you listening to? Which voice has the most influence on your thoughts and behaviour?

To listen, to truly listen, is an attribute of your Christ Self. To listen to another person in front of you and give them full attention in the present moment is such a gift to them and to yourself. As you cultivate your ability to truly listen, you will find a peace beside you. It is the peace that listens. Peace gives you a sense of the present moment so beautifully. You know how you feel when you are sincerely listened to and know you are truly heard. You automatically feel a love for the person who gives you a safe space to share. Why do you feel love toward that person? Because, in their listening, they are giving fully of their presence to you and their joining or oneness with you is total. As you give the same to others, you truly join. Listening joins you.

Now, can you truly, truly listen to your Inner Christ Voice? Will you observe the difference between the ego's loud, intrusive, fearful voice and the gentle, loving, reassuring Voice for God? You have your constant thoughts, your constant inner voices going on in your mind. Observe yourself listen to them and let the voices show you their true nature. As you hear the nature of the voices within you, the part of you that listens will be more aware of your choice to be in fearful confusion or peaceful safety.

This has been shared over and over again and is so important. This is mind-training, or atonement as we have said before. The atonement is a personal inner journey, chosen by you, of the Divine undoing of unconscious guilt and self-punishment that you have believed from the liar's voice within you. There are times when, in still moments of contemplation or meditation, you have a peaceful mind where your thoughts stop completely. You 'hear' only the peace of God, which is so delicious that you rest. You rest in God, the ultimate place for you to rest and be in the Oneness that you are. I want this Peace for you, dear one. As you listen to this quiet Voice within you, this resting in God is more and more available to you. Be still now and rest in God.

....

I hear you thinking about the 'death' of the body and wanting to know how communion between you and 'departed' loved ones happens. You do already know that real communication can and does take place as you have had experience of this. Let me share that communication on all levels, whether in or out of body, is important and Love is always the link. Where there is Love there is no separation as Love does not know about separation. Love is the great 'glue', the connector, the binder, the link in everything. It is Love that is communicating with you now and Love that you are receiving now as you write and read this.

When you think of those whom you have loved that are not with you in bodily form any longer, your thoughts are heard by them. Thought is like a language and when trained by the mind in a clear and pure way it can be very liberating and freeing, but it must be disciplined by the presence of Love. It is very helpful to 'talk' to departed loved ones as if they are right beside you, because indeed their awareness is there the moment you think of them. It is also important to forgive them so that communication can take place. Forgiveness clears communication channels and is such an important ingredient for the health of the body, mind and spirit. Forgiveness frees communication channels whether or not a body is involved. There is so much evolution and wisdom in your love connections that continue throughout your wondrous journey Home. Just because you have a body and are using a physical vehicle right now makes no difference to the quality of your eternal awareness. Do not ever use the body as an excuse that spirit awareness is not available to you. It is always available.

Conversing with me now has nothing to do with bodies. There are so many true riches through the awareness of Love's Presence. When you think of a loved one who is not physically with you any longer, they know you are thinking of them. If you, for any reason, need to forgive them for anything, do it for your sake first, and then for theirs. This clears your Love-life-line like a blocked drain is cleared. When a blocked drain is cleared, all that has been unable to be eliminated can easily flow away. Forgiveness unblocks your flow of love so you can live your True Self. If you do not know how to forgive, call on Helpers to assist you and by your genuine intention to do so, it automatically works. So much is at your disposal to use for your spirit's journey to know ItSelf. Just believe your heart and it will guide you.

Returning to communication with those who are no longer with you as a body, they certainly are not 'dead'. They are very much alive. You cannot die so you may as well forgive and love. It will eventually happen anyway so you may as well choose it now. Also, gratitude is a wondrous way to commune and feel closeness. Gratitude also unblocks the drain just as forgiveness does. Anything not flowing easily can be freed up with forgiveness and gratitude.

Many of your years can pass between thought and feeling connections from or to a loved one who is not in a body. Talk to them, forgive them and thank them. You are both deeply rewarded for this. You know from direct personal experience what I am referring to, you need no proof, but you do at times need reassurance when you doubt. Reassurance is here for you now. Love is reassuring you always.

....

74   BE IN THE WORLD BUT NOT OF IT

Here we are together, in the world but not of it. It is important to truly know what is meant by this statement. You seem to be living in two worlds.....what you experience with your body and its senses, and what you experience with your spirit. This can often be a dilemma for you but it need not be when you know what is real.

I have said before that only what is permanent is real. It is that simple. When you look around, what is permanent? Is anything physical permanent? Even your scientists who need to physically prove everything can understand permanence and non-permanence. So when you are in the world your permanent Self is in an impermanent vehicle experiencing an impermanent and often insane world.

I would like to share at this point that there is an invisible permanent Presence permeating everything within your world. This is the Presence of The Voice for God, a voice within the impermanence reminding you of your Home in God. The world you live in is not created by God. How could it be? God has been blamed constantly for the insane acts and choices of the ego/liar. The liar wants to blame God to avoid the awareness of Truth that nothing that is impermanent is real. When you can truly grasp that fact it is much easier to embrace the statement ' be in the world but not of it.' You know then that you have a choice. This choice is what I speak of often: the choice of love or fear. The liar's impermanent world is an insane world of fear, of judgement, of greed, of violence and all this is based on insecurity. This insecurity of the world is the illusion which is unreal and impermanent.

Now, I invite you to look around you (as I have invited you to do before). You give everything you see the meaning it has for you. Everything you see, even of the utmost beauty, is not permanent, is it? Many things you look at, even the sweetest of birds, are temporary. There is nothing 'wrong' with that as long as you know that there is more, that there is sight and awareness beyond what you can see with your physical eyes. This does not mean you cannot enjoy what you see, it just means to be awake to the whole awareness of who you truly are. Be aware of yourself watching or witnessing impermanence for what it is. It may be enjoyable or offensive, but only witness it. Outside of time it is only a passing dream.

I am not asking you to deny the dream or world you live in, I am inviting you to awaken to Wholeness, which is the Great Love holding you. Love's eyes see as Christ sees, which is an extension of God. Christ's Sight knows what is real, what is permanent, it sees beyond the physical dream but when occupying a body it lives in it but not of it. I speak from complete experience and my experience is also living as yours. When you know, not just believe but know from an eternal, Heavenly, knowing Source within you, as you witness your body experiencing impermanence, you can feel the Divine Love flowing all through you into everything you observe. This is bringing Heaven to Earth. You are here to bring the awareness of your permanent Heavenly Self to the impermanent world that you are experiencing now. This is your salvation and the salvation of the world. Your knowing your Self saves the world from its mistaken identity and awakens or reminds you of your true and permanent Home.

I invite you to see afresh from your Holy Sight of Love, from your Christ eyes. You cannot but help loving everything and everyone from your Holy Christ Sight for you then know Love as present in every second and in everything. To experience from the Sight of Love is your true and permanent state, it is you in your Heavenly Home. Be still now and know. Bring this Loving Knowing into the world that you are temporarily experiencing, then you can be in it, but not of it because you know your eternal Heavenly Christ Self.

....

75   FEEDING YOUR MIND

Take comfort in our quiet and close moments of sharing. They are for you because you choose to set aside times in Oneness with your Self. These times that you set aside feed your spirit and are as important as feeding your body. What would happen if you did not feed your body properly or regularly? Among other things, it would weaken. You are always at one with your Creator, but without 'tuning in' to that, your awareness of that union is weakened. Awareness is important because it affects your state of mind.

Your state of mind is what I am constantly inviting you to observe because you have to live with it all the time. Your mind is your inner gateway to your choice of hell or Heaven , your choice of fear or love, defence or surrender, attack or peace. Do you see? While feeding your mind in times of our close union you are feeding it with healthy, energetic, connecting Love Food. Just as when you sit down at your table to eat food, you also take time to feed your spirit and mind. These are quiet times in union with your True Self, your Christ Self as God created you. You make your priorities in your life and there are some priorities that are essential.

Quiet times put aside to nourish your connection with your Source are more important than you realize. It is as vital as sleep is for you. If you forget your Source, it is still there of course and you could not exist without it, but your acknowledgement of it is a great and important gift you can bestow upon yourself. You have choices in every moment, just as the use of a wand is there for you to create your dreams, your wishes and your reality. I have mentioned this before and I will again, as it is important. So you have the choice of countless ways to feed your mind. You can feed it with sadness, resentment, separation, guilt, unforgiveness, past pains, anger, hate, attack, revenge, gossip, silly dramas and so on...... you know them all. Or, you could feed your mind with connection to your Source, with beauty, love, healing, gratitude, forgiveness, joy, communion, open-mindedness and so on.... you know all these as well.

So how do you choose from the huge buffet that life presents you with? It is always there, life's buffet, in every moment, in your mind and in your sight. You have opportunities in every moment wherever you are, to nourish yourself or to poison yourself. What do you choose? Be aware of your motives in your thoughts and your words towards yourself and others. It is all 'food' in some form or another.

Our quiet times together, whether you are writing as you are now, reading uplifting words, sitting in silence, creating, connecting with your Self or being in nature, are all feeding you. I thank you for your Self, for nourishing your spirit and mind with our Oneness.

....

76   A LITTLE WILLINGNESS

A little willingness is all it takes to say 'help', to reach outward or inward and admit you cannot function alone in isolation. Your humble surrender to your Self relaxes a part of you that can truly let go at last. A little willingness is a true companion when you are committed to knowing the Truth of your Self.

What is your will? Feel it now as I ask you this question. Feel your will.... your will to live, to wash yourself, to express, to walk, your will to read and write this now, your will to do or not to do a task ahead of you. Feel your will to surrender or your will to hold back for some reason, feel your will to be open or your will not to be. Feel your will to have an opinion or to judge, or to be seen to know everything. Feel your will to be stubborn, to be set in your ways, to be close-minded. Feel your will now to be flexible, able to change and be open-minded. Are you beginning to be willing to 'get' your relationship with your will now?

I invite you to be very still and quiet in your mind right now, even quieter than you are now. Go deeper, down, down into the depths of your inner Self. This Self is beyond your physical body and matter. This is the Self you are eternally as a Child of God. Are you willing to do this? Feel your willingness or not. Let go and let God and let a little Divine Willingness guide you. All it takes is a little willingness because by inviting that, a Greater Power then takes over. This Power is a Presence that loves you beyond your understanding of Love. It has always known who you are and what is in your highest interest at all times. Are you willing to let go into this Loving Presence? If not, at least be willing to ask yourself why not. What is holding you back? What is stopping you? Your will, maybe?

I am asking you to get to know your will and where that takes you in your journey to know your Self. When you are low or depressed can you imagine a tiny light buried within you that shows itself to you and that you can follow in your mind? When you are feeling helpless all it takes is a tiny sliver of light for you to be willing to see and to follow so you can climb out of your inward hell. This moment of willingness to choose that tiny sliver of light is your ticket to Joy. But the choice takes your participation by using your will to choose. Even the tiniest bit of willingness does it. That is all it takes. I use the example of depression for a reason. You all know this state to a greater or lesser degree and can relate to what I am sharing. Your willingness is your salvation. It is beneficial for you to get to know this and use it with its counterpart, choice.

What do you feel when you are willing to unite with Loving Divine Will? Do you feel a familiar feeling of Home? Your willingness to unite with Divine Will is your ticket Home, my beloved. All you need to give for that 'ticket' is a tiny willingness to say yes from your Greater Self. What is preventing you? This very moment of having a relationship with your will is an awakening tool for you. Do you see? Being willing to read this now is enough to touch the Light within you.   I would like to congratulate you for choosing a tiny light of willingness now. Even the tiniest light of Love is vaster than you can ever comprehend and is ever-present as your constant companion. Your little willingness is that Love calling you and your willingness is responding to the call.

....

77   THE POWER OF YOUR MIND

You have no real idea of the immense power of your mind. In fact you are afraid to know, so you do not use it. Instead, you think that outside forces or agents are more powerful or relevant. This is especially the case in sickness when you use drugs to 'cure' you when your mind is actually your greatest healer. You can access the very highest Knowledge and Miracles by the correct use of your mind. It is all at your command. It's all there for you. You have been given everything from your Creator to be in Heaven now. Your choice to deny the power of your mind is your choice to stay sleeping and at the effect of the ego/liar that rules your life instead of the great awakening Force of Limitless Love.

Why are you not using your mind correctly? Now, this question does not necessarily need an answer but what it does need instead is for you to open your awareness to the fact that you are not using your mind correctly. Just to know and acknowledge that there is a stirring within you of change is to wake up to your Holy Self.

Do not be afraid of your mind, my beloved, do not be afraid of the power of your Holy Self. Allow Its light to flood you as if a dam of Light has been opened within you. This dam of Light that is the right use of the mind is awakening a sleeping awareness of your Great Self as God created you. You never left the purity of your Self, you never separated from your Creator. Your Holy and Divine Mind at one with the Presence of the 'Mind' of God is who you are. Can you take that in and digest it? Let it at least massage your awareness so you start to dissolve your false beliefs that you are helpless.

When I said, "What I can do, you can do, and more", I was referring to unleashing the Holy power of your God Self by the right use of your mind. Miracles are yours in form and non form and healing is yours because sickness, disease and pain are not known to God. Your mind, co-creating with God is one with God and always has been. All you need do is remember and awake to your Holy Christ Self that is constant and ever-present, whether you have a body or not.

I know this is still not comprehended fully by you. There is still much undoing of lies and false information that has paralyzed your Holy Greatness. This is why we write now through you, to release your awareness to another way of perceiving your Self. Either you perceive yourself as a weak, helpless victim of outside circumstances beyond your control, or you can perceive yourself as the Divine Being you really are and let the Great Love awaken a sleeping, forgetful you.

Your awakened mind is your Christ Self. Your awakened mind is your Eternal Self as God created you. You are One with the very Holiness of God. Your mind is God's mind, you are an extension of a manifestation of your Creator. I Am reminding you, I Am touching your awareness so you respond to the spark of your Christ Self. That spark then extends and extends and as your Christ Sight is used, you will know the power you have always had as an extension of the Mind of God ItSelf. Your mind is the Mind of God.

Your mind, when you think of it, feels as though it is in your head, your brain, but that is not so. Your Holy Mind is all of you, not just your body but the Whole you, the you in Oneness, in Unity with the Divine. Let these few words now at least touch you enough to open your mind and to lighten a darkness so you can at last know your Holy Christ Self.

78   YOUR CREATIVE SEXUAL LIFE FORCE

Your creative sexual life force is the force of your Divine Self expressing itself all through you. I have mentioned that your physical senses are an attempt in your body-form to replicate your eternal Heavenly awareness. In the same way, your powerful sexual desire in your body is an attempt to replicate your need for Heavenly Divine Oneness. Your sexual desire is actually your Divine creative life force but it is misrepresented by the ego/liar and has been wrongly directed. In its essence, and this is not easy to put into words, it is the ego's great power to keep reproducing itself as a body when in truth the higher use of your sexuality is to co-create with God.

In using sexuality only to temporarily satisfy a body-ego desire, you are missing out on the Great Power to Divinely co-create. This does not mean you cannot enjoy sexual union, it merely means that your sexual desire is so much more than it seems to be. It seems to be a force so strong that it cannot be ignored. When it is 'awakened' at the time of bodily puberty, if it is taught to be directed creatively with the presence of love, it can be your awakening. What have I just said? Your sexuality can be your awakening? Yes, when you accept and know you are more than your body, more than the sexual desire forcing its way into your very veins. Pause...... watch..... see it for what it truly is --- an awakening force. Do not be blinded by its seeming attachment to the body. This attachment to only the bodily needs is the clever trick the ego uses to keep you in forgetfulness.

You are not like an animal that is only at the mercy of its bodily instincts. You are a spark of the Divine with the use of a temporary body that is reminding you of your power as a co-creator.

When you want to wake up to what your sexuality is really for, you will unleash such power of Love that your Joy will almost overwhelm you. Your body sexuality is, at best, a reminder of the God Power permeating all through you all the time. It is your great desire to co-create with your Maker and unfold your eternal Life Force. At worst, your body sexuality is a monster that you can witness which has blinded and seduced you into thinking it controls you so that you let it temporarily destroy your Holy memory of your True Self. At worst it is in complete control of only your body so you forget you are eternal spirit. At worst it crucifies and creates pain, destruction and separation. You can witness this all around you in your world.

When you know what your bodily sexual awakening really is and step aside from attachment only to your body and its 'needs', you have the ability to have a total spiritual awakening at puberty and not only a sexual one. In the teaching of Truths, mystics throughout time have known this and used their God Mind to teach and train themselves to use the body's sexual force to unite with the awareness of Love's Presence. This is true initiation..... the union of body, mind and spirit in Knowledge of the Great Creative Life Force which is your birthright.

Your sexuality is not wrong, it is just misdirected. When directed correctly with the right mind, sexuality opens you to your Magnificent Self. This has been known and used correctly and when it is, there is never any need for any kind of false images, fantasy or misuse of the imagination. It is a gateway to Love and Holy Relationship in the true sense of Oneness. It is not a false understanding of love resulting in the experience of separation, loneliness and isolation.

If you want to know the power of your creative sexual life force it will teach you from within. It is all within you. You are not the victim of your body desires, but the co-creator of your Divine Unfolding. I realized this and I was not immune to the power of sexuality in my body. I welcomed it and I witnessed it as you can do. Watch it and where it wants to 'take' you. Only watch, witness its force, its power and at the same time be aware of a much Greater power, the Power of your Source. I surrendered my sexual power to my Source Power, not completely easily at first, I must admit. My Source did not take away my sexuality, it merely directed it through right-mindedness into its true state. In a body I enjoyed sexuality as a tool of love and union with another as well as knowing the union and co-creation with my Divine Self. This is also available for you. It is not as difficult as your ego wants you to think it is. It is, in fact, totally natural. In the surrendering to a Greater Force, your sexuality is such a gift for your Spirit in Joyous Oneness.

....

My purpose here and everywhere, that I share Truth, is to help you live in the world in your original state of Heavenly Oneness. All it takes is a change in the way you are experiencing, in other words, in the way you are aware of everything through the filter of your mind, which is your perception. For example, if four of you were in a room observing the same thing.... say, a spider weaving its web in a corner, each of you would see the spider differently from the perception you have of spiders. One might be in fear, another in awe, another might think to get rid of the spider because it shows the room needs cleaning and another may observe the spider from the spider's point of view, weaving its web as its home and as a net to catch its food. None of you is wrong or right. You are merely watching and experiencing the spider from your own unique viewpoint or perception. Now, let each of you try something by changing your 'sight' of the spider from human eyes to your Christ eyes, from worldly sight to Divine Sight. Now, how do you see the spider?

Your 'homework', your going-Home-work, is to change the way you perceive from the ego/liar to Divine Love. This change of perception is the miracle moment you give yourself to know your true Christ Essence. Every moment of your life you are perceiving, whether it be the way you think or how you see something, and how you are feeling in the moment determines the way you experience. Personal perception, in other words the way you individually experience, is based on many factors and these can be your beliefs, your education, your interests, your environment, your wounds, your passions, your culture and so on. This is natural in the world you live in. However you are not, in essence, any of these things. You are not a victim of your worldly life as much as you might think you are influenced by it.

You are more, so much more, than your day-to-day perceptions. You are Divine, you are Christ, you are Love incarnate, you are as God created you, not merely influenced by outside circumstances. Do you feel this? Do you feel how much more you are than you seem to be? In an instant you can choose to change your perception, your experience of anything, by remembering who and what you truly are.

I Am here to help you change your perception from an ego-worldly one to a Loving Heavenly one, from fear to Love, from mistrust to Faith and from a belief you are separate to the knowledge you are in Loving Oneness. I Am here to remind you of your True State as God created you. All it takes, my beloved, for you to do this is a change of mind, a change in the way you perceive everything in every moment. Are you a victim of the world or are you a co-creator with the Divine? You have this choice in every moment you are thinking and in every moment you are experiencing yourself.

Watch yourself. I keep asking this of you. Watch your mind, your beliefs and your actions. You are not stuck or stagnant, you are free and flowing. You can step out of attachment and watch. From the watcher, the witness, the observer, you are able to perceive differently. What part of you is watching? And what greater Force is witnessing you with such Love? Even those very words broaden your perception.

Let go of any perception you have of me, Jesus, from any past stories. I Am a reminder of your true Self as part of you that is united with that which created us in the Great Oneness of Love. I Am here, more than just inside of you but ONE with you to help you change your perception of the upsidedown, insane world and to see from your Christ eyes the true Heavenly world that is your Home. It is all in the eyes or the perception of the beholder. Now behold your Christ Self and everyone around you through the awareness of the unconditional, generous, all embracing Love that you are created from, and be aware of being in the Presence of God.

....

80   JOINING

Joining is aligning with, uniting with another and that is what we are doing here, now, my beloved. I invited you to join with me when you asked who you truly are and together in this Holy Sacred Time we are united in Love. Within this unity in Love you are remembering your Self. I want you to join with me, the Christ Self, to know and remember your Christ Self. In this joining we are One, as is our true identity. Joining brings us into the awareness of our eternal non-dual Oneness as we 'stand' in the Presence of Light and let that Light shine on and activate our True Divine Minds.

We do not join in a body sense at all. We join in our mind. This is what we are doing now as we write and read together in this moment. We are joined in a communication which takes place in our One Mind. Your mind and my mind are joined or united in Love's alignment and we both give and receive from the same Christ Mind as God created us and this is the very experience of our original creation.

When we join, the I Am in me knows the I Am in you and we know our One I Am. Joining brings you into alignment with who you truly are and then automatically aligns you to whomever you are with. To be truly with or present with another is a mental unity first because when two minds are in alignment they share the same communion. It filters from the mind into the body when you are physically present with someone.

This brings up being in communion with those not in a body. I Am sharing these Holy Words of Truth to remind you of your Whole True Self. When someone drops their body in so-called death, they do not and cannot drop their mind. You can still join with them and they with you. What do you think we are doing now? What we can do, all can do and what we are doing is joining minds in Holy communication. Any so-called mystery of death is dissolved when you realize you can always join minds. This is important to know and experience because you can have a false idea that without a body you cannot communicate. Yes, the body can be a communication device but the mind is the origin of communication or joining.

I love our unity as it is the flowing way we are naturally and lovingly being together. It is natural, maybe not 'normal' in the temporary world's experience, but totally natural in your Heavenly one. It is totally natural for you to join in Love and Oneness. It is not natural to separate in judgement and defence. We are in Love's One Embrace together and setting time aside to do this together in your world is one of the best ways you can use time and feed yourself.

I 'feed' you with my awareness and you receive my 'food' of Love and you are deeply nourished with such a full experience of remembering Love's Presence. Here we are, my beloved, joined in Love, in Peace, in Truth and my function is the same as yours: to live in the awareness of Heaven's Holy Home.

....

81   BLESSING

A blessing is a gift from your God Self. You can all bless because your Christ Self is your God Self. You know about blessings, you have given and received blessings often. As you bless, whether you recognize it or not, you are using your Eternal Spirit and recognizing in your Self the Power and Love that you have and are.

It is a beautiful gesture to bless another and even to bless yourself, because you are giving from your Essence. Even when you say to another out of habit, lightly, 'bless you' you are reminding yourself of the Presence that you are capable of accessing. To access this Presence that is always yours, willingly and consciously, is a wonderful blessing and gift to yourself. You all have an equal, endless Presence of Love permeating through you. Even as this is mentioned now, it is felt, is it not?

This Presence of Love is not static, it does not stay still for it is moving, interacting, giving and receiving constantly. It is creating, co-creating, witnessing, breathing in and out, and is alive all through your body and spirit. When you give or receive a blessing you are consciously using the Presence of Love. This Presence is meant to be used, meant to be shared and communicated through and towards you. You are accessing your God-Christ-Self when you bless anyone or anything and you acknowledge the Power of the Divine within you. You are flowing in your True Essence, as is your birthright.

Right now, bless the pen that is writing this and the hand holding the pen. Bless your eyes as you read and your mind as it interprets these words. Bless your heart for centering you in Love. Bless your awareness as you look around and bless your thoughts as they may be Christ thoughts. Bless your mind for its power as you use it rightly and your life as you know it is a gift to access your Creator. Bless your ability to Love and to receive Love. Bless your Joy as it runs through your being.

With your eyes, silently bless everything and everyone you see whether you know them or not. Do you feel the Presence of where the blessing is coming from? Are you remembering your True Self through the power of blessing? The Power you have is accessed as you bless and as you receive blessings. When you look at yourself in the mirror, bless yourself and feel the gift you give yourself. When you bless your food you are changing the very molecules in your food to align it with the power it has to nourish you. You eat then from a higher state because you have, through blessing, remembered your Heavenly Mind.

Blessing is of Heaven and is automatically bringing Heaven into everything you bless. The blessing of your Creator is running all through you as your very breath. Everyone has within them the power to give and receive blessing. No one person has any more right or 'power' above another to bless. You are all able to be in a blessed state. To be in a state of giving and receiving the blessing of God is being in a state of Grace. You could even replace the word blessing with Grace. Try it.

Look into a mirror and say to yourself, " I bestow the Grace of God upon you." Know what you are accessing as you do this. From gracing or blessing yourself you can grace or bless all others and all things as you bring the awareness of your Source into that Holy Moment. Blessing changes the moment from being mundane to being Divine. Remember now to bless, to receive blessings, remembering what you are accessing as you give and receive. You are in the Presence of the Divine and you are the Light of Love. What a true blessing you are.

....

82   THE BIGGER PICTURE

The Voice for God is your connection to your True Self. You know you have two different voices in your mind and you are choosing between them all the time. Sometimes you watch them and sometimes you are too attached to watch. When you are too attached to the voice in your mind you are often tense, angry, frightened, threatened or defensive. The ego/liar creates an attachment with you that says it needs to protect you, but that is a lie, for it is only protecting itself. The world you live in is a result of the lie that says you must be protected by outside means in order to be safe, hence wars, the constant build-up of weapons and separation, and you do the same thing in your personal life. However there is another voice, it is the Voice of Love, not the ego/liar's voice in you mind.

This is why I have asked you over and over again to watch, to observe your thoughts from a place of non-attachment. Just watch. Then you can choose cleanly because, as you watch with no attachment, you have a clarity in your ability to choose. You can view the bigger picture from the watcher. As you see the bigger picture your unity with your Christ Self or Higher Self will be clear to you. You can choose anew, you can surrender to the Love that knows the very highest for you. Do you feel this? The presence of the watcher within you is like the Sun, shining unconditionally and constantly on anything that stands beneath it. The Sun, the Light is your non-attached awake Self witnessing the 'dream' from outside of it.

The whole experience of being beside yourself, watching instead of the attachment which is being at the effect or the victim of everything, is important for your peace of mind. The busy defensive mind must be still when you watch it because it hates to be seen, for then its lie is exposed. Watching your mind is exposure but the ego/liar does not want this and is very clever at avoiding it. The ego is very clever in trying not to allow you to see your True Self.

Oh, my beloved, as we write now we are exposing the ego/liar for what it is..... nothing. It is nothing pretending to be everything. Truth calls to you from your Eternal Self and uses your Sight to see from your Christ eyes and from that sight makes a choice based on Love. As you undo false thoughts in your mind that you have believed about yourself, you are making space at last for the Voice for God within you to be heard. This undoing is a choice. It is your atonement. The moment you make this choice to undo all that is not true, the love from your True Self attracts Helpers from all realms to help and be beside you. Your little willingness to be as God created you is your salvation. The Helpers' sole job is to inspire, remind and guide you. I Am a Helper and am in the company of all the angels of The Big Picture. You are not alone. There is always the bigger picture and it sees from Love's Sight.

You have many thoughts about yourself and others which start in your ego mind as ideas and then extend and become stories. You have the ability to create any story you want to about yourself and others. You can create a story that you are poor and you need this and that 'thing' so you would not be poor any more. You could have a story that you are a victim because of this or that and you are helpless. You can extend that victim story as something that has happened to you in the past which you cannot do anything about and that is the reason you are forever stuck in the emotion you experience. You have a poor-me story about ailments and aches and pains in your body.

You could have a story that you cannot accept certain words because of their link to religion or misuse of power around them. This can be a major story for many because certain words like God, Jesus, atonement, redemption, Holy Spirit, Miracle, sin and other words push buttons that you find uncomfortable so you avoid anything to do with them. You have stories about Jesus that are from the past and bar you from allowing me into your heart as part of you now. You have story after story that you have believed and made part of yourself all your life. Now, I am not saying all this is wrong. I am just bringing your awareness to some of the various stories that you may have.

You can change any story and make it into another story for yourself, a positive and creative one. I am rich, I am healthy, I am happy, I am free, I am as God created me. There are all kinds of stories you share with yourself and others. The point here is, which story is honest, true and uplifting, reminding you of your True Christ Self? Who is creating the story, your ego/liar or your Voice of Love? There is a point when you go beyond all stories and truly live what your story is. Which story do you want to live? Misery or Joy? Fear or Love?

I have told you that I Am not the Jesus of the stories that you have heard. You might have needed those Jesus stories to recognize me, but I ask you to let them all go and in their place I am telling you that I am the same as you....Christ with no story except the expression of Divine Love itSelf. The One True Love Story.

This is a Love Story of you remembering and uniting with your True Self. I Am that Love Story and have embodied it completely. Now, as part of you as our Christ Self I Am living the Love Story of our Oneness through you. We are in Love, living the experience of Oneness as our Christ Self. Letting go of the blocks to Love's Presence is letting go of any other story. This is beyond any story now because your ego mind is not in charge of anything and instead our joined mind has come into the awareness of the One Christ mind as it has always been.

....

For many, many years in your world's time you have been influenced by authoritarian institutions that have used words to feed guilt and shame within you. Through this influence, sadly, you have associated certain words with self-punishment and self-hatred, causing more guilt where these words could actually help and heal you instead. Guilt is keeping you away from remembering your True Self and this has been through forgetfulness and by those in authority feeding your sense of guilt. It is the ego/liar at work, and I Am here to correct your mistaken ideas about yourself.

When over and over again you have heard the words, " Repent for you have sinned", or "You are a sinner therefore you must repent" or " You must atone for your sins", you have been given words whose false meanings have entered your innocent, pure and sensitive mind to make you succumb to a false power or authority. This, at last, is being exposed now in many ways, as you know.

I would like to emphasize once again that you are innocent, you are pure, you are still as you were originally created by the Divine. Repent simply means 'think again'. Sin means 'mistake' or 'off the mark' (an archery term). So when you are told to repent for you have sinned you are simply being invited to think again for you have made a mistake. Can you let go of old attachments to words that have caused you to forget who you really are? Can you change your mind or re-think a mis-taken belief that you are guilty and not worthy of God's Holy Blessing of Love?

Atonement is simply choosing to drop or eliminate anything not of Love, and this is something you choose for your own remembering of your Christ Self. You have been mistaken or been asleep (sinned) and you are letting go, thinking again (repenting). You are awakening to what has always been and what is Real within the Knowledge of your Christ Identity. You can at last let go of past associations of misrepresented words that have fed your guilt and forgetfulness. Let them go and free yourself of guilty feelings or thoughts you have had about yourself. This will lighten you in every way.

God is not judgemental, heavy, unloving or a punisher. You have never been and will never be punished or judged by your Creator. There is only Love there for you and it always has been. It is just up to you to clear the blocks in the way of that Love so you can receive it. The ego/liar has created God in its own image and in its own words. This has been the great lie I was exposing when I walked the Earth as Jesus 2000 years ago and this is the lie I am still exposing.

The Truth is in my resurrection and yours, my beloved. Your resurrection is your full awakening to your Christ Self. Anything in the way of that is false and creates guilt and fear within you. You can be sure that when you are aware of fear or guilt in any form you are seeing it for what it is... the ego/liar. Then you think again from that mistake and know the Truth within the depths of your being. The

Truth is what sets you free. It is within you and always has been. I Am merely reminding you of Truth, of Love and of your Holy Self as Christ.

....

NOTE FROM ALICE

For the past few transmissions I have been watching myself from 'somewhere' while I am writing. I have been observing myself as I write, at one with part of myself. So today I asked the question:

"Who is writing this?"

Answer: Who is writing this? I Am. Myself asked for my Self, so my Self, the I Am that I Am is answering myself. It is all within me as I have told myself. Who am I? I Am. I Am is writing and I Am is naming this I Am, Jesus Christ. I Am Christ writing to the part of myself that has forgotten who I Am. I Am communicating and joining by invitation with all of myself. All of me includes the part of me that seemingly separated, yet, if the separation was real I could not be having this communication now.

The thought of the separation extended and became the ego world I seem to live in now, yet it remains only a thought, only a made-up part that is not of God. There are thoughts of and from God as well as unchecked, unreal thoughts going through me   from my 'separated' ego self. Which thoughts do I want to align with? Which thought system, the thought system of God or the thought system of my ego, am I choosing in every moment?

I accept the atonement for myself. I accept the undoing of the false and sleeping part of me so that I can remember the I Am which is the only motive in these writings. I Am undoing anything in the way of I Am and have all the help of Heaven for this to unfold. I Am blessed, grateful and loved. So be it.

....

85   WHERE YOU PUT YOUR ATTENTION

Where you put your attention, there too will be the manifestations of your life's intentions. At this moment, as you read this, where is your direct attention? Pause and be aware of where your attention is. Now, is this awareness from your Christ Self or your ego self? Is your attention from love or fear?

Your attention is from the mind's 'sight' or thoughts. It is your priority and values. Your attention can have motives, stories, emotions, conclusions, justifications and so on. It can also be in the experience of joy, love, peace, gratitude, faith and so on. What are your priorities? Just observe in the quiet time of Now what your essential priority is. Your essential priority is what all else comes from. Feel your priority in your whole Self now. Does it serve your Christ Awareness? If not, are you willing to create and commit anew? If so, watch this as you are aware of consciously coming from the Christ that you are. You have such help, more than you could ever realize, to know your True Self.

Where you put your attention is also your Inner Altar. Your altar, both inner and outer, is your point of attention and intention. At this moment see in your mind's eye your Holy Inner Altar. Feel the power of this focus and allow it to be a mirror for you to show you where you are in your awareness. Observe yourself from a loving, non-judgmental 'place' as you experience your Inner Altar, your focus of attention. Now, re-commit to your Self from the Source of Inner Peace, of True Knowing. You DO know, you have always known your True Self, your origins. As you now give this knowing your attention, any forgetfulness dissolves and Love reunites your attention with your True Christ Self.

Oh, my beloved, what Peace and Joy are yours when your attention is on the Truth of your Holy Being. This is Grace embodied by you, dear Christ.

....

86   **NOW**

Here I Am Now as part of you in the Oneness that we all are. As you remember and embrace your Christ Self, you are coming Home to your true, Holy Self. You are Holy, you are Divine, you are Blessed and you are Love Incarnate in this and all moments of Now. You are remembering and within the remembering a quickening, a stirring is breathing through your heart and spirit. It is actually happening to all beings whether they know it or not. The time to know your Self as the Christ Presence that you truly are, is Now.

Now is all there is. You have heard this before and there is total truth in that statement. Now, this Holy Divine Now, is outside of time, space and even mental understanding. God knows nothing of time as you know it. God knows nothing of space as you experience it. You have a memory of knowing as God knows, it is Truth and pure Knowledge and you have always had this within you. You are as you have always been..... you are as God created you, all else is illusion. You are now eliminating what you are not so you can embody the knowledge that you are and have always been the Holy Creation of Love ItSelf.

Oh, my beloved, I Am passing on my awareness through these writings as we unite in the Oneness that has forever been ours. In this Holy Now all is remembered and known by you. Keep the awareness of the Holy consistency of the Presence of Love all through you. Your Gratitude, your Joy and your Heart extend the Love to your Self, then to others. This is the way of being your true Christ Self. This Now is all there is and all there ever has been within the eternity of Divine Presence.

Yes, it is vaster than understanding, vaster than words can express, vaster than your mind can grasp in its present state yet Truth is forever embracing your awareness from its Holy Source. In this Now as you read this, surrender to the Source of your Self. Each

Now moment that you do this you are giving yourself the greatest gift you possibly can , for you give yourself your Self. The reality of this blessing is everything. Now the Divine is really embracing you forever in Holy Love. Now God is smiling with you eternally. Now is the reality you have always been seeking. Now is Christ living through you, and you know this.

....

87   STILLNESS

In this Holy moment let us surrender to stillness. This is more than an outer stillness, it is an inner one. The stillness I Am referring to is the quieting of your mind. A still mind is a treasure for your whole being because within the stillness you have a Divine space and are aware you are as God is. Yes, you are as God is and this is your true and natural state.

Let us now know the Divine Self that we are in the stillness. Be aware of your consistent breathing, just gently aware of it. Be aware of your still body and your choice to be in this Holy time with the God that you are. Here, the peace that goes beyond understanding embraces you like an eternal hug of such Love that you know you are always safe and secure. This stillness is as a great pause in habitual activity and anything that has taken away your attention of this peace is dissolved away.

Stillness is simply being. There are no expectations, no past regrets, there are no fears or worries.... it just is. How refreshing and renewing is this stillness. As you are experiencing the stillness, watch it. Somehow, the being in it and the watching are the same, are they not? So, stillness is the watcher. The watcher is always still, no matter what is happening.

To be aware now of the stillness and the watcher as one being is your renewal, your healing, your vantage point for Knowledge. This stillness is an active force of God's Presence. It is permeating you eternally and it is in this moment as you are watching it that it is being made known to you. You can bring this into every moment of your life, consciously. You can bring stillness into thoughts, into activities, into communications, into creativity, into relating and so on. The stillness of your inner being is your core, your eternal essence. From this core you are in the center of your Self. Your Christ Self lives here eternally and radiates love to and from you.

All through the day remember your stillness. In the act of remembering you are automatically embodying it. Stillness is your Self embracing you with everything you are. Now, you are at one with your Christ Self.

....

88   COMMUNION WITH YOUR CREATOR

It is your true nature to be in complete communion and communication with your Creator. You are not meant to be frightened of your Creator, you are meant to be in awe and ease with knowing you are the Child of the Divine. This is your Christ Self in

Oneness with Its I Am. I Am is in reverence, in Love, flow and mental union with that which it is extended from. You are an extension of God, within God, so why should it ever seem difficult to communicate with and receive communication from your Divine Maker? This is the way I converse all the time through the power of mental union in the same way that I Am communicating with you now.

Put aside quiet times to 'call' your Maker as you would call or phone your mother or father for wisdom, advice and Love. Your Maker is your Mother/Father who loves you beyond human understanding. I invite you to totally trust that Love. The more you have faith and trust in that Love from your Creator the more you will flow as your true Christ Self. You can use the representative of God, the Holy Spirit, in whatever form you want to speak with God. The Holy Spirit is the Voice for God and this Voice was given you at the moment you seemed to separate and forgot who you are.

When you ask, you receive. When you pray, you are answered. When you have the trust that you are loved, you are alive in a way that lights you up from the inside. My beloved, the Light you are is meant to shine all through you and also meant to witness the experience of others' lights. What you are experiencing then, as light beings communicating with each other, is the use of your Christ Sight, your True Sight.

Can you, for a moment in your imagination, take my hand and walk a little with me, in your mind, to a quiet grove. Here we sit together and join in our common goal to commune with God. God knows all you are going through, all you need, all your joy and pain. God also knows the bigger picture of your Self. Please completely trust that this is so. In this sacred space you are surrendering to your Holy Self that has never left you and as we commune together you remember and know your union in God all through your being.

This is why we are here. This is why we are writing and reading this now. The I Am that you are is God's Holy Creation and is embraced in the knowledge that you are eternally living in Love. This communion is charging the battery of your soul's awareness and you can take this awareness everywhere you are in the faith that you are so loved.

When you know you are truly loved you have an inner confidence with yourself. That confidence can extend to loving others because of Love's limitless generosity. To receive and give Divine Love is your destiny and your gift to your Self. It is your true nature to be in complete communion and in Love with your Creator. Now that you know this, please use it. Use it in your thinking, your actions and your awareness.

You are in the blessing of Love's Holy Presence eternally.

....

Right now, experience a miracle--- a change of mind and of thinking. Know with no doubt that you are as God created you, Christ, God's Holy Child in your original innocence, in your original moment of extension from your Creator. What power and strength there is in this knowing. You are everything that is of your Creator, being the extension of Holiness ItSelf. Take this into your deepest core knowing for it will 'trigger' your total awakening because as you embody this there are no more excuses to be asleep or unconscious to knowing your True Self.

From your True Self you are the embodiment of Miracle ItSelf. To be miracle-minded you are Christ-minded. Your whole Self is at last in its rightful Holy Mind and from your Holy Christ Mind you see, feel, know, live and embrace your life as your Creator envisioned. You are Home.

This Home is where you have always been but have forgotten. It is the miracle that loves you as you return to your Self. It is instant, outside of time and always available as a simple choice. Choice is not difficult even though the ego/liar in its   pride may convince you that it is. Choice is instant and uses the easy access of miracle to direct your knowing in awakening to your Self.

This knowing is surrounded by the glory of the Light that shines on Truth. It is truth that sets you completely free from false beliefs that have confused and hurt you. The Truth is totally surrounded in

Holy Love and is the breath of healing in everything. Miracle and Truth are embraced in Love and are yours for the asking. When you ask for a change of mind from fear to love, from sleeping to awakening, from doubt to faith, you know the miracle as your companion. It has been created as part of the Wholeness of your being so you cannot deny that it is there.

Any false denying you have done to yourself has only brought confusion and pain which is not necessary except to show you what you are not. The purpose of pain in any form is to bring something to your awareness. Pain in your body makes you aware that something is not in Divine order, is amiss and needs the Holy Hand of healing. Pain in your mind also reminds you that something is not in Divine order. Mental pain is a torture to your soul. It is reminding you that there is another way of perceiving or looking at a situation. This other way is the miracle way, the miracle path of Christ-mindedness,

Here we are, my beloved, healing any pain you may have in any moment by reminding you of the instant remedy.......Miracle.

....

90   YOUR CHRIST SELF

What is truly meant when I tell you that your name, your identity is Christ? What is Christ and what does that imply? I have stated that you are Christ, as I Am. I Am Christ and the I AM that you are is also Christ. Christ is just a word on one level, so we must go beyond the word to the meaning, then beyond the meaning to the knowing and then beyond the knowing to the experience of becoming. Christ is the Holy Child of God eternally created by God, and you are that. The name Christ is given to whom and what you are. In knowing and remembering your Christ Self you become it, yet you need not become that which you have always been! So by remembering and becoming Christ, what you are doing is embodying the reality of your faith in knowing you are the Child of God.

Once you remember this, everything changes because in full knowledge of your Source all thoughts, perceptions, and feelings can only come from this Source. All else is false and from a liar in your mind that you have believed, and this false belief has stolen your inner joy. Only you can recover what you yourself have given to the thief of Truth. You have been deceived by forgetfulness.

In reclaiming the awareness of your Self as the Child of God, you see and experience everything differently. Doubt turns into faith, sadness to joy, tension to patience, death to eternal life, guilt to innocence, fear to love and all 'sight' becomes your Christ Sight. This discourse is for your remembering. Your inner teacher whom you have chosen as me, Jesus, is really the Love you are as your Self.

In reality, this is very simple as it has always been, only the liar/ego has covered up the simple truth with confusing and complicated lies of deception. It is all in your mind and as we have said over and over again, all it takes is a change of mind which is the miracle. You are the living miracle for your Self. No one, no matter how close you are to them, can do this for you. You are responsible for your own change of mind, your own miracle and the owning of your Christ Self. Yet by the miracle you automatically affect all others because of the connection in Oneness.

This is Love in action, God in the Holy embrace of Oneness with you and everything. As you own the awareness of your Christ Self you automatically know your Oneness as Wholeness and you extend that by living as Christ. I know, I have experienced this and now I pass my experience to you and you and you. We all now know that we dwell in Heaven eternally in God's Home together as Christ, God's Holy Child in the original innocence we were created from.

Oh, Holy One..... your Christ embodiment goes beyond your physical body. It is of course the eternal life of your spirit, your light, your very Source itSelf. Rejoice now in the full knowledge of your Christ Self. You are so dearly loved.

....

91   VIGILANCE

You are taking into the core of your Self the remembering of your true and original nature, your Christ Self. It is my purpose, my destiny, as it has always been, to walk beside you and help awaken you and all beings to their Self as God created them. It is one thing to know this intellectually, it is another to commit to it with your Whole Self. This commitment must be total to be effective and that means vigilance.

Vigilance is staying awake. Sometimes this is easy and natural but there are times when it is not so easy and does not seem so natural. Vigilance is your inner witness, your watcher and your choice to stay in the awareness of God's Holy Presence, your Christ Mind. You can be fully committed, which means a thread of total surrender runs through your deeper Self, yet daily there are distractions, surprises, tests, shocks, illnesses or words that divert your clarity. This is natural and this is what is being worked on in your mind training as you are the watcher of your thoughts, actions and feelings.

When you are watching yourself from non-attachment you are being vigilant. Vigilance also means choice which most of the time will be easy for you because by now you know the consequences of your choices. I must remind you, however, how clever the ego/liar is and how insidious it can be at justifying itself. Your mind is accustomed to witnessing all the effects of the liar in your world, for the loudness of its presence is everywhere. Your moment-to-moment choice to see with your Christ eyes and not to judge with the eyes of your ego is with you constantly. You must be vigilant.

Even so-called enlightened beings have been known to come under the spell of the ego/liar. It will not let go easily. You have helpers, you have connection, you have love surrounding you eternally yet you must constantly use your power of choice through vigilance to help yourself. It is a moment-to-moment choice, as I have said before, each moment to be in Christ Awareness. You are doing very well, yet you know when you have judged another for your own ego's delight! You know very well when you have allowed your anger to become exaggerated so it can feed itself. You know very well when your choice has been not for the good of your soul.

I could say this is normal or natural because you are only human, but I will not use that excuse. It is not natural even though it seems the norm. You are not only human, you are temporarily using a human body but you are not your body. You are eternally the Holy Light of the extension of God. The Light that you are is vast, brighter than your sun and it is total Love in Heaven's Holy domain, yet you have forgotten it. Be vigilant for who you truly are.

Your vigilance is your very loving companion helping your commitment and choice to always be who and what you truly are. I still have my companion, Vigilance, with me and I always will. True Vigilance is Love guiding you and it always has been. It is helping your choices and lighting your way. When you know that Loving Vigilance is part of your Christ Self you will be more at peace in your mind for your mind knows it has a helper and is protected.

Go well now, my beloved, in your Christ Awareness, committed to your Self with the Angel of Vigilance by your side whispering reminders to you when you are tempted to forget.

....

What name do you know me as? Jesus? Yeshua? Yeshua Ben Joseph? Jesus Christ? I use whatever name that you can directly relate to so we can unite. Ultimately I Am and that is enough. I Am Christ and you are that also, yet beyond the name is what is and together in what is we are exactly the same. We are the same because there is only One. This is the heart of the Truth and your Christ Self..... the one Child of God.

More and more people will be writing, speaking, and teaching in my name and using it to embody their Christ Self. You will recognise the loving message as the same because it is. The carrier or scribe may use their own understanding of words to express this message. The time is now and I Am using Now for your awakening and for the awakening of all beings in the Oneness they truly are.

We are undoing, we are eliminating as we unwind all the illusion that duality has seemingly created. We are at the beginning with no time, a paradox , I know, but words cannot explain no time, no space and non-duality. Instead of words you must float in Love's trusting realm and experience Oneness as it is. For you to do this, everything you have related to in your world has to be altered and experienced differently. It must be experienced through your Christ Mind which is the perfect extension of God's Mind.

The world as you experience it in duality is a split world and so you experience everything as separate. God's mind 'sees' nothing as separate. All is in the One. This may be hard for you to fully grasp or understand so I ask you to let go of any need to understand and to simply accept. In acceptance of what is, you are free of any need to understand.

So, even my name, Jesus or Yeshua could be taken on by you in the acceptance of your self. Ultimately, if God was to give you a name it would be Christ-born-of-Love. For the purpose of your self-recognition it is important you know the Christ Love that you are because it embraces the deep memory of your origins.

My beloved, you are as you are, name or no name. You are as the One Holy extension of your Creator and slowly you are knowing this again. Everything comes from this and nothing else. Accept this and all else unfolds in the harmony of Love's Truth. In the denial of your Original Self you have believed in the separation from the Holy and Innocent essence of your Being. All is well, you have actually never really separated in Truth. All is well, your Oneness is guaranteed.

....

93   THE ABSTRACT

I have mentioned before that words are symbols of symbols. At the same time they are being used here to take you beyond words to an experience. I use words in the case of this discourse to trigger a memory beyond words, beyond time, space, understanding, form and concepts. Here we are now in the realm of the abstract. Abstract means formless, among other things, and God is formless, abstract.

It is in this abstract realm that you can surrender to the vastness, the eternal Presence of the Divine.

The abstract is not of this world. It is not of matter, touch or the body. It cannot be seen or felt in the normal sense. Abstract is out of the body comfort zone, which is perfect because that is exactly where we need to go to experience your Christ Self. The ego/liar is not comfortable in the abstract because it has no space-time reference. My beloved, there is only one reference for you, and that is your Creator. One is all there is and God is Oneness, as you are.

Allow yourself now just to float in the loving abstract Presence of your Divine Creator. Let go of anything you know about your body, thoughts, feelings or mind. Allow Love to transport your awareness to Love, outside of anything you know. The formless is something that is not unfamiliar to your spirit. After all, your spirit is formless.

You seem to be in a body form now, using your hand to write this and your eyes to read and your mind to absorb these words in this moment. This is a type of form, and you know as we write together in Oneness that your experience goes beyond your everyday knowing. Form is not permanent and nothing impermanent is real, so what is permanent? What is endless and timeless yet present eternally? You know and you have always known. It is the complete non-dual Oneness of your Self as God created you. In the awareness now of the abstract even the word abstract has to melt into Oneness.

Spend a little meditative time surrendering to the abstract Presence of the Divine now. Let Love take your 'hand' and let the Peace of God be your guide. Here we meet in formless unity as One, the I AM.

....

94 LIGHTNESS AND HUMOUR

There is a saying, "you can go to the depths of hell and if you laugh nothing can touch you." There is great wisdom here because as I have mentioned before, hell (and Heaven) are states of mind, not a place. Hell is the way you perceive something in your mind. If you can imagine or recall a time when you might have been very depressed, that is a state of hell. If you could laugh then, how could depression touch you? A sense of humour is a light in the darkness, or a lightness in a heavy situation.

From my observation, most people take pretty much everything too seriously. When you take things too seriously that always means there is attachment and any kind of attachment to anything always causes pain. There is so much emphasis on attachment in the world, which is a way of keeping the separation alive. Attachment can be to things, people, bodies, ideas, beliefs, and even a false idea of yourself. To give and to receive in Love is the rightful flow of energy and the way life flows easily. When there is too much attachment to anything there is always fear.

My beloved, you and most of humanity take everything far too seriously. It is so healthy to be light, to be humorous about most things. This lightness not only keeps you happier but also puts a healthy perspective on the impermanent, transitory nature of situations. Of course, there are times when some situations call for a serious concentration and focus and we do not deny this but remember always to be the observer and to witness. When you witness you cannot be too attached, so any emotional, mental or physical pain can be diminished.

From the perspective of those who have left the body, when they watch those still on Earth they are often shocked at the attachment that seems so normal in the world. Attachment and taking things too seriously can be heavy and I ask you to 'lighten up'. When you lighten up you are more open-minded and happier and a sense of humour can be found in most situations.

For a few minutes, go within and think of people you may know who seem heavy, attached and too serious about everything. Feel how you respond inwardly and outwardly to them. (I am not saying that there may not be a time when it may be appropriate to be serious about something, I am being general here.) Do you find it more difficult and even uncomfortable to be around people who show this side of their behaviour, for whatever reason?

Now think of those you may know who are joyous, light, non-attached and less serious about everything. How do you respond in their presence? Where are you in this? What would you like to be.....

heavy and serious or light and humorous? They are both a choice. You can use your attitude to something as a yardstick to your state of mind. Watch yourself as you would watch from outside.... I invite the witnessing and watching for a reason for it is the non-attached way to know your Self.

You are not meant to be so attached. You are meant to watch, choose and experience the result of your choice. Your choice to be heavy and serious or light and non-attached through humour is something I just want to bring to your attention. Life can flow in child-like wonder when you do not take things too seriously, and this is the state of your Christ Self.

....

95   COLLAPSING TIME

Many times in my various communications I have referred to collapsing time so it might be a good idea to enlarge on that. Time, as you know it in your world, does not exist in Heaven. Eternity is not about time. The world you live in uses man-made time, or man-defined time and also man-defined space. The time you use and never seem to have enough of has nothing to do with the realm of God. Time in your world causes separation, stress and seems to define birth, life and death. It is used as part of the ego/liar to keep you in amnesia.

God's 'world' or Heaven knows nothing of your world's time line. It is timeless, in the eternal Now with no beginning or end. I know it may be difficult for your earthly awareness to understand this but it is so. The Holy Spirit goes between both Heaven and the world you live in and is available to remind you of Heaven, your natural state.

When I refer to collapsing time, what I Am talking about is bringing a timelessness into your timeline to eliminate some of your time so you are aware of Heaven as part of your whole being. At the moment, Heaven or the eternal awareness of Love, is not part of your day-to-day awareness but when it starts to seep into you, time as you know it becomes compressed. The 'wheel of Karma' or the hamster wheel of birth, life and death will stop at last.

This wheel of birth, life and death is not the True Whole picture, thank goodness. It is the liar's way of keeping you locked into illusion, or separation. I enter your time to tell you that there is no time! Your open-minded Christ Mind knows this and can bring no-time into the world's time and this is the realm of miracles. Miracles collapse time because they work completely outside of time. Truth is outside of time and when you access no-time, or God's eternal realm, you truly know the domain of miracles in everything, just as you have always been meant to.

So, eternity collapses man-made time and transports you to the only place that is real..... Heaven. Even now, as you think of Heaven you are there in your mind. You can use the thought or awareness of Heaven in your everyday life to bring miracles that are outside the realm of your world into your everyday living. How wonderful is that? Yet, it is the norm as you live your Christ Self.

When you can include Heaven's eternal now as a reality in your life you collapse your known ego time-line by huge chunks and are closer to your Self than ever. This is one of the key ways for your

Christ Self to know ItSelf. I can take you, as I am   doing now, into Miracle Mindedness and then all Divine attributes are yours. This is your birthright and always has been. Your true Christ Self lives in eternity and witnesses worldly time dissolving as you are more and more aware of your Home in Heaven.

....

96   AT ONE WITH YOUR SOURCE

You are at one with your Holy Source and you cannot be otherwise. This present moment is here for you to claim your origins once again and know your Holy Self from your most Sacred Source. You are eternally connected to the Love that created you. You are eternally connected to the Peace that created you. You are eternally connected to the Light and Joy that created you. You never have not been. You have merely temporarily forgotten your connection, your unity and Oneness.

Here we are, my beloved. I walk beside you on the Starry Path to your awakening. All you need do is to know who walks with you as you wake from the dream of illusion and forgetfulness. Then you will know your Self as you are.... Christ in Divine Oneness with your Creator.

"What went wrong? " I hear you ask. You played with a mad idea and then invited your mind to believe it. Your mind believed you to be separate from your Source and so you have been witnessing the experience of forgetfulness ever since. However, it was only an idea, only a mad idea that you separated. It is not real. Reality has never left you but instead you mentally left it. This is why we unite here together now, in Love, to remind you who you are and of your eternal connection to your Source.

God, your Source, wants perfect happiness for you always, and you will be in that state as you know your Source. Your connection is your salvation, your Wholeness, as it has always been. I take your hand and your mind as we unite now in experience and I show you the connection we both have as the One in Unity and Completeness. We are complete in our Source and we can never forget this. All illusions of time, of cycles of birth, life and death as you know them, cease to exist outside the illusion, outside of the lie that separation has convinced you is truth. How can suffering be true when you are created in Perfect Love? How can death be true in any way when only eternity is real?

I invite you to pause. Be still and know your connection to Source and who you are in that. You are your Creator's Holy Child. Your connection is whole and perfect and all is well. The awareness of your Christ Self, the extension of your Source, is present more than ever before for everyone to truly remember and truly know.

The time of awakening is NOW, even though it may not seem that way in your insane world. More and more people will speak in union with me for I Am the Truth and the Awakener for you all to know your Self as the same as I Am. We are the Child of God in Holy Oneness with our Loving Source.

Within the realm of Christ Sight, Heaven, there are no contradictions, no opposites, no anger, no fear, no mistakes and no need to forgive. Yet forgiveness cleans your eyes so you may see with Creation's Sight. You were created as One, in One, to know Wholeness where there is no reason to forgive because there is only the Christ Being as you were created by God. This is always with you and always has been. Your Christed Self is who you are, innocent and whole in the sacred Sight of your Maker.

Do not let the clouds of forgetfulness obscure your awareness any longer, my beloved. The sun that shines in constant Light does not disappear because the clouds of illusion are temporarily in its way. Let the Light of Truth shine upon your heart to open it as it becomes once again what it is meant to be..... the reflection of the Original Love you are made from.

Your Holy Heart, your eternal spirit Heart is forever beside your physical one, touching all you are and it calls forth a healing of the mistaken thoughts in your mind so that you can know your Self. Then your heart and mind unite once again in the memory of their original Oneness in Love's Holy Place of Peace. A peaceful, loving mind is God's mind extended to your own. This is your Home, this is your origin, this is who you are in your Christ Awareness.

I Am emphasizing your Christ Self here over and over again because I Am calling forth your deep memory of your Creation in the formless and limitless realm of Heaven. Words can only go so far to guide you there in this moment. Now we must go beyond words while still using them.

Your Holy Self knows where to go now because your commitment and willingness have given it the strength and life force to do so. Your strength is Love and your life force is the strength from your Creator flowing all through your mind. Your mind now is in its correct place, One with God as it has always been. If ever you waiver from knowing this, remember your Love, Strength and Light and breathe the breath of Miracle. Then you will know.

I Am always here to remind you because I cannot be whole without you, for we are as Creation made us in the perfect reflection of ItSelf in Oneness.

....

98   YOUR LIFE IN LOVE

Soon now this book will end, but your life in Love will never end. You wanted to know who you truly are and I have told you in simple words used over and over again in different ways. It is important that you re-read this often for it is undoing all you are not and feeding your memory. You are like a newly born baby born into the awareness of yourself as Christ. Your newness is really your original Self created in innocence and all Knowing.

Yes, you know and you have always known your Self. Hold this in your awareness always. You may observe your separated self and think you have a long way to go. I say to you that you are already in your Life of Love. Your thoughts of any lack of your True Self are only passing clouds across the Light of your Knowing.

Suddenly it will all make sense and this dream will be forgotten quickly as the illusion it is. Remember to watch yourself. This will help you so much and will also keep you non-attached and in lightness. You are not at the mercy of your forgotten self, you are the Presence of Greatness beyond your understanding. Your life now is to keep on keeping on with your growing faith in your Self. Never forget you are as God created you. Be what you are in honesty with your mind's highest intention. I Am here to guide you all the way Home.

....

99   I AM WITH YOU ALWAYS

I live within you always. God lives within you always. Your Christ Self lives within you always. I have said that you need no intermediaries or anything from outside of you. It is all within you and always has been. I AM a reminder, a mirror for you to remember and then use what you remember. Your Christ Self is your true Self and who you truly are. Are you getting that now? Are you able to access your Self and have trust in Its loving consistency? This is what we have been doing here, my beloved. You asked, and here I AM. It is Divine Law that when you ask from your genuine Self you are always answered from the Truth.

It has been said over and over again in many teachings that the Truth is within you, and it truly is. Never, never think for a moment that you are not worthy or ready for the Truth. God does not acknowledge or even know of thoughts such as these. God's total Love is who you are and that is enough. You are enough.

Please now be aware of any diversion or pull you feel you have to seek outside of Your Self. You may need temporary guides to help you become familiar with your inner terrain but then even they can be dropped. Any true guide or teacher only shows you the way to your Self and then celebrates your awareness when you no longer need the guidance. You are on your way to your Self in Joy. Even though I am communicating with you here, we are equal in our experience of Oneness. We are together in Heaven, our Home, and can observe easily from this awareness.

Keep observing, witnessing yourself from your True Self. Behind the observer is the Watcher, Love ItSelf, guiding you in perfect Peace. You know this now. You are on the Starry Path and there is no turning back. You are on the path and at the same time you are in the awareness of your destination, Heaven.

This is your 'course', your journey with me to remember your Christ Identity, your True Self. It is always available, always present within your Self. This is not the only reminder. Truth is so generous it always gives and gives to you in different ways . These words have been for you because you asked. Take them, use them, ride with them, they are your stars on the path. They are stars of Light until you need no more stars. You recognize the Star you are and you guide your Self in every moment of Love as you live as your ChristSelf.

....

100   WHAT NOW?

What now, you ask? Are there more writings? Do we have more to share? My beloved, I AM always here, in Heaven's time to be with you in dark moments of forgetting. Your mind has now been triggered to remember but the ego is not wanting to give up so easily. Your separated self is in the close embrace of your Christ Self and it will need that closeness daily. Just ask, and I will instantly be with you because I cannot leave you. We are connected as the Original Self that extended and created us in Its own image of Oneness. I am you. When you need me, you need your Self. Never doubt your Self. It is true and has always been as it was created by God.

Each moment continues, each now moment you can witness from that part of yourself that is not attached to the drama and story that the liar wants you to believe is you. You are awake and you have to stay vigilant for God and the True You. You asked to know your True Self and you committed to that. You asked also to help others know their True Self. Your journey, your course, is given you to follow and know. You can put your course out to the world because you are not separate from anyone and they are not separate from you. As you give, you are given to. To give and receive are one in Love. In giving you receive. In receiving you give. This is how Love is.

Put this simple course out into the world and those that are drawn towards it will read it and remember. Re-read it often, for your own sake, so you can share awareness to help others know that their answers are within them. So be it.

....

THE PRAYER OF THE CHRIST SELF

My Christ Self that is eternally in Heaven,

Holy is my name.

I will know My Self on Earth as

I Am Christ in Heaven.

This now is always in the embrace of Love.

As I forgive those whom I feel

have hurt me in any way

I am instantly healed and forgiven.

I am vigilant as I watch and recognize

the ego/liar in my mind,

for Love is my true Guide

and Source eternally.

AMEN

EPILOGUE BY JESUS

I Am here with you always. As I have said, when you need me you need your Self, and you do need your Self. You need your Self because your Self is who you are and wants to be the expression of your magnificent Self....... and it is magnificent. You all are as your Creator made you, nothing less. In forgetting this you have given up your Self to an impostor that is only a tiny fraction of your True Self.

You have believed a lie that has convinced you that you are little and that you need outside, man-made authority to guide and control you. This is a total lie. The Truth is within you. I am a mirror of the Truth and the magnificence of who you are. Now is the time that the lie is exposed.

There is a saying, " Where there is a spark of the Holy Spirit the ego/liar comes and organizes it". Authoritarian, dualistic religions on Earth can be hypocritical institutions. 'Religio' or religion means 'to bind you back to the One'. This does not mean binding you to man-made laws but to bind, to connect you to your Creator, your origins, to bring you back to the One which you have never left in truth. The One you were created from in Love.

I am not a Christian, I am bound directly to my Creator. If I were to assign myself to a religion it would be called Love. All-inclusive, unconditional, open-minded, joyous Love. Love is the great connector, the binder. It is not the divider, the separator and the liar. Remember, my beloved, your magnificence in your Christ origins and your eternal golden connection to Love.

It will take time to undo what for lifetimes you have lived and believed. That time can be greatly condensed with your willing choice to know your True Self. Receive now your inheritance of your shining magnificence as you allow the Presence of your Christ Self to live in you.

NOTE FROM ALICE

These times I have spent in communion with Jesus have been so easy. All I do is 'show up'. I often say, ' Here I am, Lord' and then quieten myself. With a pen and notebook nearby I am ready for a communication. First He comes to me through my thought channel and all other thoughts are silent. Then, I take up my pen and write the thoughts he gives me. He uses my vocabulary and often even includes a topic I heard recently, about which I might need some clarity. He gives me more than clarity, He gives me the whole loving Christ perspective! It is simple and easy as He uses the language of images and shares a lot with me through joined experience.

Often I have been in the middle of something, cooking or going for a walk and I have no paper and pen with me when He starts talking to me in my head. I know it is Jesus because of the Presence that comes with Him. My mind chatter stops and He takes over, gently and oh so lovingly. When I write later we pick up from our inner conversation.

I know this being called Jesus is really One with all of me. It is as though He is also the Christ that is My Self. It is so familiar and I am at Home in this Presence.

I have asked Jesus if there is more he wants to share and write. His answer is yes, definitely, but not until I have fully taken in all that he has given me so far. He tells me that there will be questions from myself and others for Him. In the meantime, I recommend re-

reading His beautiful words over and over again. The energy in the words can massage our hearts and help us unwind untrue perceptions and redefine our identity to be in our True Self.

....

I was recently asked "How do you know this is Jesus?" So I went to Him and asked the question and this was His answer:

"What part of you is asking this question? There is no need to justify or to question when deep inside you know.This has been asked because you have been challenged by someone. That is normal and others will challenge you and ask you the same question.

I AM not the 'Jesus' of stories, I Am the Jesus of the I AM, eternal and at one with God, as you are. I Am not identified with the name, Jesus. I am identified with Christ. It is the Christ in us that is communicating and joining here. Just as you are temporarily Alice in this incarnation but Christ in permanent eternity, I Am and that is everything, as you are. Of course you will be challenged. I was challenged and am still being constantly challenged. The truth is eternal but the liar has tried to define and mold it into its own distorted perception, and separation has occurred between the children of God. Wherever separation exists you know it is not Truth.

I Am using your hand now to share and write with you, for you and in you. When you come in quiet, still moments to converse with me, I AM there in the way you can receive easily. It is Love that is writing. You can replace the name Jesus with Love. I AM Love-Christ and in our union so are you, so is whoever is reading this now. I AM beyond the name Jesus, it is only used to access Love, my beloved.

You are more than Alice, you know this and yet names seem to be needed to identify or even to feel familiar with. You are beyond any name, even the name Christ. I use it to identify a quality, a knowing, and then we go beyond any names, identifications and words. We write in Oneness with what is. The Holy Presence of Love is with you always."

CPSIA information can be obtained
at www.ICGtesting.com
Printed in the USA
LVHW051033020520
654894LV00019B/1534